The Language
of the
Psycards

by
Berenice

The Language of the Psycards

©1999 Berenice Watt

Psycards copyright Network Ltd
Artwork copyright 1989 Maggie Kneen

ISBN 186163 056 5

Cover design by Paul Mason
incorporating Psycard designs

Published by:

Capall Bann Publishing
Freshfields
Chieveley
Berks
RG20 8TF

DEDICATION

I dedicate this book to my children, Nicolette and Colin. I thank God for giving me two children with such incredible understanding of my path in life. I thank my children for giving up so much of their childhood time with me to allow my work to flourish.

TO IAN

Thanks are so inadequate to give to someone who has been a continued loving support and, at times, a bulldozer in the background - in order to make one get on with the work!

TO GORDON

Thank you from the bottom of my heart for introducing me to Psycards.

TO RICHARD

To whom I also owe thanks, without his help this print run would never have happened.

CONTENTS

THE WISDOM OF PTAHHOTEP

Fifth Dynasty, c. 2500 B.C.

Do not let your heart become proud because of what you know;
Learn from the ignorant as well as from the learned man.
There are no limits that have been decreed for art;
There is no artist who attains entire excellence.

A lovely thought is harder to come by than a jewel;
One can find it in the hand of a maid at the grindstone.
Do not let your heart become swollen with pride
In case it may be humbled.

It is true that one may become rich through doing evil,
But the power of Truth and Justice is that they endure
And that a man can say of them "They are a heritage from my Father"
If you are resolute, acquire a reputation for Knowledge and Kindliness

Follow the dictates of your heart.
Let your face shine during the time that you live
It is the kindliness of a man that is remembered
During the years that follow....

ORIGINS

Personally, my first contact with Psycards came at the Mind Body Spirit Exhibition, Olympia, in 1984 whilst l was working as a Consultant for the British Astrological and Psychic Society. A colleague asked me to do a reading for him with his own cards - Psycards. Although l had never seen them before we clicked together immediately - the result was that, by way of thanks, I was given a present of a deck of Psycards by Gordon Smith (the 1987 Chairman of BAPS).

Following this introduction l commenced selling and demonstrating the cards around the country. However, I was as intrigued as anyone else to know where the concept of the cards originated. I wrote to Network Limited with my query and here below is the reply I received, which I feel is very relevant and explicit:

Dear Berenice,

Psycards were developed in 1981/2 by Nick Hobson and the cards were drawn by the artist Maggie Kneen.

Nick Writes:

"I'd long had an amateur interest in the Tarot pack and in the psychology of Carl Gustav Jung. Being an introverted sort of person myself, I was always trying to work out what made myself and those around me tick. The actual concept of Psycards came to me - believe it or not - in a dream. My wife had at one stage chucked me out of the house and I spent an uncomfortable night on a friend's sofa. In my dream I saw all the factors that made up my personal life - my background, my work, my friends - spread out before me so I could move them around and perceive the relationship of one to another. When I awoke things at last seemed clear and simple and the idea struck me for

Psycards. I was lucky to find a marvellous and talented young artist to interpret the idea.

Maggie Kneen, who was influenced by Anglo Saxon art and culture, worked with me on the symbolism of each card. Our aim was to create something pure and beautiful, but simple which would help people of today understand themselves better at many different levels.

I know for a fact that some people have psychic gifts (I myself do not) but I believe the cards can be used by people in all sorts of different ways."

Thus, you have the origins of Psycards themselves, but for the 'origins' of the Language of the Psycards, I suppose you must look to myself and my years of involvement with the various dimensions of life together with my family background. My parents, who both passed into spirit during the final stages of the preparation of this book, gave me from babyhood a spiritual understanding of the many psychic happenings that we experienced. My mother was a spiritual healer and had mediumistic abilities, so when I had visitations, insights, foresight and downright ghostly experiences she was there to explain or show me the way to understanding. As the years have passed, I have been lucky enough to have had personal contact with most spiritual/psychic manifestations and have found that Psycards can be a natural extension to the senses. When I am asked to explain this, I find the easiest way is to express that Psycards have become the clairvoyants' pictures for me since I progressed away from that way of working many years ago.

INTRODUCTION AND CONCEPTS

As you will probably realise, there are many books on the market covering cartomancy, giving various theories on the meanings of cards and their positions. No doubt you will expect this to be another of them however, it is hoped that by the time you finish reading this book and studying the cards you will have come to a completely different conclusion.

I have always believed it is far better to allow the Psycards to introduce themselves. Once you hold a deck in your hands begin to come alive, they warm to your touch, they almost reach out and speak to you before you commence to look at the individual cards. As you begin to look at their pictures they start to communicate with you in their own subtle way. '

4

Psycards open to you a new field of experience from whatever position you are in life. Their design is to catch your imagination and open it to fruitful speculation on different aspects of your life. Their charisma appears to be hidden from view, but once you hold the cards it begins to reveal itself in their colour and quality of perception from within the depths of yourself. Allow them to become an extension of your self, feel them harmonising with your true being, let their life enter your mind and become the outward picture of that which is truth. The designs and pictorial images touch wave notes within your deepest memories. Then the colours dance before your eyes, magically triggering even deeper memories and emotions. In this book, I have to put that essence into words in a manner which will introduce you to the cards and the background of their special spirit of life.

Firstly, I must emphasise that in reality there is nothing magical or mystical in Psycards unless you include in that word the understanding that all life is magical and can be mysterious. The pictures, as you will see, are simple, clear, and to the point. They direct you to the variety of events, emotions, and people in life generally, thus the real magic in the Psycards is Truth. Their concept is to assist you to gain a greater insight into yourself, initially, by helping you to be truthful with yourself - thus wiping away the cobwebs that slip over our personal vision; when this has happened you will find it easier to help others go through a similar process.

Psycards are not designed to tell fortunes. They are a way of opening up your awareness to the variety of opportunities that lie around you Psycards will show you all your past mistakes - how to change the pattern of your habits and thus your lifestyle.

Many will try to bring in age old concepts and symbolic meaning, plus numerology. In this book I have tried not to interpret the cards in set meanings for you, but, as previously implied, tried to guide you into using your own psychic intuition along the pathway, using the cards an extension of your eternal self.

Throughout life there are facets which are the same whatever nationality, creed or sex you are, and these permeate from similar causes. Therefore, incorporated within the pictorial imagery of the Psycards are the themes which can be seen in any divinatory tool, but there the similarity always ends. Other divinatory tools always cling to the past, to previous magically symbolic features to put themselves over to the public as being special.

Psycards are for the New Age, and although their pictorial facets are ageless, their process is to take one forward into a new way of thinking. You will find that Psycards not only open your mind to different areas of your material and emotional self, but finally trigger off the opening of the psychic capacities, which everyone has to one degree or another.

Psycards have been produced in love, with a love of colour, art and mankind- thus you have a deck of cards which respond to love, and will love you back from the beginning. This explains the feeling of life within the cards when you actually hold them. To add to this, meditate, or gently clear your mind, and quieten yourself down each tie you hold the Psycards prior to using them.

Meditation is also a good habit to develop. It is a simple way of attuning yourself to another level of Self and a further dimension of life. This process need only take a minute, but you will find that better results are obtained. Meditate on the pictures, let them come alive in your mind so that their meaning for you becomes personal and fluid to suit your needs each time you use them on the journey/voyage through yourself. You should aim to let the eyes just drift over the picture and fall on whatever they will, so that your inner self directs your gaze.

There are forty cards in the complete deck, and as the aim of the Psycards is to assist us in control of our own self, you could say they represent the mystical forty days and forty nights Jesus spent in thewilderness after which He came out in control of the Self. Here, I also give a few more thoughts to help expand your ideas before using the Psycards. Taking the number 40 as 4 + 0, it equals four, which represents the physical earth plane and it is on this material plane that we seek help, since it is the dimension in which we are manifest. Note also the four elemental qualities - Earth, Air, Fire and Water; and then the four aspects of self - Physical, Astral, Soul, and Spirit. Within the number four we can find the digit two, symbolising the dual aspect.

There are five indicators which are separated into one plus four; and then five groups of seven cards each depicting a different aspect of life. Here we can define the number four equalling success, it is also the number of solid matter, practical application, self-discipline, strength, and is considered a sacred number, since many ancient cultures use four-lettered names for God. The numeral five equates with resilience, individualists, philosophy, organisers, and is a halfway point between nought and nine - symbolising the past, then future within view. Seven represents the studious, creativity, artistic judgement and dreams; the colours in the spectrum and notes in the musical scale; also the seven major chakras. The digit one is our Inquirer, all alone - the start beginning, self. Finally when five merges with four as in Psycards with the Indicators and Groups together, it is a signal of nearing completion.

Incorporated in the main interpretations of the cards you will also find simple meanings for the colours within the concepts of Colour Therapy and Auric Interpretations. However, the explanation for each colour will not be repeated throughout the book, so there will be a need to refer to the listing at the back of it, in Colour Interpretation.

Naturally, Psycards are meant to be fluid in their interpretations; therefore, in time you will find your own meanings and solutions to the cards from their personal language with yourself. When you are reading the individual small-example spreads under each card's title, please remember that my personal professional life is dedicated to a full time (seven days a week, usually) working knowledge of the cards. Add to this my experience as a mediator between various dimensions of Life, dealing with spiritual and practical facets, and as such I have tried to include the variety of connections which I have experienced as being associated with each individual card.

As with any divinatory tool, a decision has to be made before the cards are laid, such as to past, present or future positions, in order to facilitate easier interpretations. With Psycards, it is also not difficult to switch levels within the reading from either the material life to the spiritual aspects if so wished; this can be done prior to the cards being placed or during the actual process. It is usually simpler to actually have a special position incorporated within the spread for the card(s) which may be clarified on this level. You will also find the placing of additional cards within any spread adding new meaning to each individual card - together with its specific position.

In order to really expand your awareness and understanding of the Psycards you must allow your intuitive and sensitive side to flow forward. But, ask yourself; what is intuition? Is it that 'sudden knowing'? Where does intuition come from; does it come from the mind? What is the mind? Can you hold the mind as you can a brain? You know it is there, it works, and comes from somewhere - just like electricity, you cannot see it but you know it is there and you can experience it. There are many things in this dimension which we now accept but do not have sight of. Remember, people who are physically blind cannot see electric light but accept it, and those who are physically deaf do not hear music but accept that it exists. Learn to stretch your imagination and awareness then try not to dismiss something out of hand just because you have not yet experienced it.

Now, even if you are going to be using the Psycards for your own personal expansion and use, you are still classed as the "Reader" in this book. Your question/problem or situation in question becomes the Inquirer or Sitter. Therefore, I emphasise that within the terminology used in this book consider yourself as the Reader and your cards as actually being laid for another person - the Querent; by doing this it will enable you to step back from the situation and assess the lay objectively.

Naturally, the views and expressions used in this book are there to assist you to expand your own vocabulary and points of view on themes. The paradigm of each card is like a kaleidoscope reflecting the avenues of life; therefore, let yourself become the reflection of it. There is always a need to study the cards, noticing all the time details which in turn may be interpreted. The time may come, however, when your eye alights on one small detail only during a reading, and this is all that is necessary to give a solution to a problem. We do not, therefore, always need to speak about every aspect of a card at every sitting.

One last comment; in my opinion the art of becoming a good "Reader" is to develop your ability to sense clearly the way in which your 'physical' sitter can accept messages and information so that any kind of topic can be touched upon with ease - we all understand differently and react emotionally in a variety of ways. A responsible attitude must always be developed when dealing with other peoples' lives, together with an ethical code of confidentiality between sitter and reader. The best way to develop this attitude is to accept every reading, whether done in fun or seriously, as private, personal, and professional.

Finally, remember when you go to use your Psycards for the very first time, hold them in your hands and let your mind slip down into a meditative state, allowing your thoughts initially to clear. Then let the formulation of what you require of the cards to grow in your mind such as Truth, Guidance, Accuracy, and ask for protection - the protection of the Universal Light or whatever you perceive as the Ultimate - God.

THE CARDS AND INTERPRETATIONS

INDICATORS

Here are the first five cards, which I have drawn together under the heading of indicators, since they do not sit within the general symbology contained under the headings given to the Main Five Sections. However the Indicators are also split in two by the fact that the first card has been designed to stand alone: The Inquirer, which is you or the question.

The importance of the INQUIRER Card becomes obvious as soon as you begin to work with the cards, so I have therefore dealt with it separately. Then there are those which are drawn together under the title of the Direction Cards. Within all aspects of progression through the complicated and various states of life's situations, we come across times when clear-cut direction is required; thus the Direction Cards are borne with their initial meanings: YES, NO, NOW, and NEVER. So, therefore, initially use the cards simply as their individual titles imply, as pointers directing you to or away from a particular course of action and as straightforward answers.

All of the Indicators are exceptionally important when a question needs to be answered in a fairly straightforward way, yet as you become practised in using your intuitive/psychic self, you will quickly be able to use these cards as fully and explicitly as the rest of the pack. I believe that, as you read through the themes that I have found progress from a variety of topics involving this section of cards, you will be able to use all of them fluently instead of taking out this group as I have seen so many do, thereby using every single card fully as a key to the Language of the Psycards and your own subconscious.

1. THE INQUIRER

As you gaze at the Inquirer, the intricacies of the card are immediately obvious, the main pattern giving thoughts of the aerial view of a maze. The split base colouring of bottle and lime green shows the negative and positive sides of green, which relate to the states of your mind. The overlaying of the clear grassy-green gives the impression of the maze, which is interlaced in the centre with a ribbon of brick-red being interpreted as, within the concepts of Colour Therapy, aggression and harmony, thus bringing together a complete pictorial symbology of a confused state. We also find that the border of this particular card reflects the thoughts of opposites, together with a maze in the colours of yellow, red and sea-green.

Initially the card itself - in its pictorial imagery and title - states that it represents you, the Querent and the questioning state. It has firstly been designed to represent you in this way, within a pattern of cards to assist in interpreting a solution. However, it is also a card which can stretch the mind and pose questions in itself.

The normal use of this card is as the significator, thereby governing the reading from the position where it lands. The Inquirer card will mark the centre of the situation and the point from which a layout should be read, but generally it must be remembered that this card represents the person making the inquiry.

Naturally though, this card may be used in the same manner as all the other Psycards in that it can, as you may already have realised, be full of meaning in itself, which can be simple or of total complexity as is the labyrinth of life. Oneself can be seen as a maze - half darkness and half light, yin and yang, out of which it is essential to seek the centre. Yet dark and light are also coexistent and dependent upon their counterpart for their own definition. How can one appreciate goodness without having experienced at some time it's opposite? An answer is often there but lost inside your head or heart, on another level within, through which the seeker has to search in a downward way; it might be unpleasant of conversely very enjoyable. There are many patterns formed in one's inner world which are projected onto the outer. Therefore, one can be hemmed in by one's own set ideas yet a certain amount of harmony can be derived from a state of order!

This card may merely point to the inquirer's mental, emotional, or psychic levels being in a muddle; or physically lost in an area like Hampton Court Maze! However, it may be the complexity of the world which has caused you to get lost on your pathway, and this card stands for that point where you need to try and perceive an answer, by going within to find a quietness from where you can think clearly. To go within a form of meditation (see relevant chapter) - just allow the pattern to draw you deeper and deeper.

Another way to use the Inquirer is to make it the focal point for concentration and allow your psychic/intuitional side to develop, thereby giving the correct individual meaning for the Querent.

2. YES

An intense diaper pattern of various shades of blue, with a splash of bright red in flowers together with black linework flow within this card, and often you will find yourself drawn into its depths. The positivity of the answer from this card is also within the colour interpretation, as portrayed in the red and cobalt blue flowers, bringing vitality and purpose together in accord to create action towards balance.

Here is the first of the Direction Cards and one which is very important in our lives - Yes. How many times do we look for that confirmation as to whether we are on the correct path and have taken the right decisions? The interpretation could be left there with this card purely meaning YES - Go ahead, an affirmative answer, the proverbial green light. However, as you will no doubt appreciate, there are those occasions, when in difficult situations, the need to know that your intuition is correct arises and the answer is 'Yes - do not go ahead', therefore, it is necessary to expand upon this card's uses.

Generally, the Yes card gives you a favourable outcome to a situation and tells you that you should be optimistic about the future changes in question. The position of the Yes card within a divinatory display is exceptionally important, and will definitely assist one to define the fullest interpretation. For example, in a four card line up question regarding a health condition, should The Body, Yes, Beast and Sun appear in that order, it would imply that the condition would deteriorate before getting better. In this instance, therefore, the Yes is positive but with a negative flow as well.

As with all the Psycards, the patterns displayed in this card are ideal for meditating upon, especially the method in which you are attempting to train the mind to be still.

3. NO

The second of our Direction cards brings us, once again, black linework defining a diaper pattern in red and blue; however, the slash of blue is almost lost in the overlay of reds illustrating the colour consciousness interpretations of blue for devotion, being swamped by the red of greed, hence the need to stop!

Since 'No' can be a very negative and pessimistic vibration, it is essentially advisable to use this card only in a spread, whereby the adjacent cards lend flavour to its full interpretation. The majority of us look for an explanation as to the reasoning behind the answer to our question when it is given as no, and the additional card(s) will show this. Yet the 'No' card alone is simply the red light, a blockage, the indiction to stand still and hold back. Therefore, when expanded upon, it generally becomes a card which is telling you to beware.

As with all cards, the actual position in which the No sits in a layout assists with its definition and is, therefore, important. It may sit in the position of the past, present or future, and since it can be a very negative card it is imperative that you can define whether the negative phase is passing or not.

Obviously, there maybe an indication given in the layout that there is a need to change one's negative outlook or attitude, and if the No lands in the future position, the signification may be a barrier or obstacle which has to be overcome. Here again, an excellent card for meditation and one which can be used as a mandala. Bringing forward an awareness of colour again, and its usefulness - if you are feeling under the weather, as they say or tired, use the card as a focal point for a healing meditation by concentrating upon drawing the red of the card into yourself and then allowing the blue to finally balance.

4. NOW

Still with the Direction cards, you will see the flow is towards the following sections in that the design is now including a scene.

Here we have the impression of a stained glass window brought about by the leaded light effect of black lines forming the diamond patterned background, but interspaced with a blue flowered orange and yellow tile effect, the three colours bringing forward the interpretation of inspiration, material and mental alertness respectively.

The rest of the window effect is created by the rays of the sun laying across one corner, but seemingly shining down upon a farmer wearing the green of regeneration and brown of earth practicality. In his left hand, he holds a scythe cutting the ripe corn to stack in sheaves. All this illustrates pictorially the vitality and positiveness of action.

The card initially means the time is right for action since conditions are favourable.

There are many indications of flowing phrases within the picture, and I have tried to incorporate a few together here. The time has come to take in the harvest of that which you have sown; there is a sense of reaping goodness, although it needs to be remembered that the harvest does not always come up to expectations; the hint of the sun brings feelings of better times to come, yet the scythe gives a sensation of a need to cut something away first.

The stained glass window effect can bring thoughts of a church together with implication of the religious harvest festival service and its predated 'pagan' rites, thereby perhaps indicating one should give thanks for that which you have received up to now.

A further definition in this card may be deciphered from the circles in the background which link with cycles, etc. The squares refer to a balanced foundation; however, also shown within the squares are triangles which imply, in esoteric terms, the Trinity.

Naturally, within a spread the meanings here may be found in the reverse; the intuition may signify that there is a lack of balance; lack of thanksgiving or even a lack of reasons to be thankful for. It is, therefore, important to look at the surrounding cards.

For example, if the question is to find out whether it is the correct time to change a job and the cards are - The Cave, Now, The Wheel, Work and the Message - the indications would be that 'Now was the time to change, that in the past there was nothing to be thankful for, yet now was the time to cut free and look for success in the future!'

5. NEVER

A dismal card full of dark dull colours, a black raven, the largest and most despicable of its kind, even to being cannibalistic. The bleakness of this card is extended from the winter snow-clad branches into the background. Although the pattern is somewhat pretty, the colours of various greys and muddy orange, in colour interpretations, give fear with dullness of imagination and lack of intellect to describe a wasteful time which is fully indicative of the reason for this card.

The initial definition of this card is simply derived from its title - Never - purely implying that it is never going to be the right time or correct decision. It definitely gives a bleak outlook riddled with failure and thus denial of fulfilment, therefore, can be more final than the No card, yet this, again, can change depending upon where the card is positioned within a spread. The card is indicative of delays and warnings, since life always has its darker side; there is a need for symbology of this within any divinatory method. All sides must be shown and the Never card truly draws out the harder side of life.

Here is the pictorial display of a warning of impending failure and devastation of ideas or situations. Also, there are the times when we have to be cautious of the scavengers in life, yet in another way this card could imply that you should awaken to the moments in situations when you are the scavenger of your fellow man. To expand upon this card's interpretation, study it within a variety of questions shown in layouts, when it can also imply the reverse of what has been written here. It can then indicate that your worst fears may never happen.

In a layout where the Destruction is in the past position, the Never sits in the present and peace is laid in the future, the elucidation would be simply that the devastation and failures of the past would not happen again in the future. Thus there can be a positiveness about this bleak card.

Since the colours and pictorial illustration are oppressive, it is not generally a card upon which to meditate. Obviously there are extreme cases when it can be interesting to do so, i.e. if you are strong willed and wish to find out more about your own oppressive nature!

THE FUNDAMENTALS

The Fundamentals cover the basic qualities that are so important to us and are significantly apparent in everyone's lives. These are the aspects which comprise the foundation patterns of our development and growth throughout life in this dimension.

As can easily be seen, if you lay these cards down together, the pattern emerges appertaining to our background and environment in an everyday manner; we need correct BODY functions to develop SKILLS in order to WORK and earn MONEY to create a HOME and true FORTUNE is in FRIENDSHIP!

6. THE BODY

The diamond diaper linework of the last cards continues faintly here in the background design of bright blue and pink enlarged veins. However, the pictorial concept which was developed slowly over the last two cards now comes boldly to the fore in the form of a body outstretched. The theme of the background is expanded upon in the main design, in that the body and limbs are stripped of skin, allowing the muscles and veins to show. The basic colour therapy concepts here are the radiant blue of healing and the red of the vital life force. Initially, of course, this is the card of health, fitness and energy - or lack of- but then there are many other key words which spring to mind such as physique systems, tension, vitality and meridians.

We require, firstly, our body's rhythms to flow freely in order that our heart and other muscles function correctly, thereby allowing us to enjoy life, whether it be in a working aspect or through hobbies. Here again, thoughts of sports and dancing come to mind, whereby we may turn to the need for all parts of our body to work properly and be free of injury in order to serve the whole.

Let your eyes drop into the body shown in this card, so that you may be drawn to a particular area, such as a leg or shoulder, indicating an area of bad health or damage, such as a tendon or pulled muscle. As you progress with the development of your intuitive abilities, there will be thoughts as to whether this is a current condition or a past one, although the position of the card in a spread will assist with this, as already suggested. There may be an intuitive impression that a general building up is required by way of exercise, or perhaps vitamins and minerals are the call of the day. It is wise also to remember that irregular blood pressure is a condition relevant to a lot of people, but one must be gentle and cautious; therefore, do not be too dogmatic as to the precise condition. However, with continued use of the Psycards, the intuition is naturally developed and expanded, thus your interpretation of the varying aspects of this card will grow.

Energy flows and patterns also come to mind; not just the energy loss taken for granted when exercises have been overdone, but the Universal Force that flows and can be sensed within the spiritual healer's presence.

This force is known as 'Ki' in Japan, 'Chi' in China and 'Sekham' in ancient Egypt. The awareness of the meridian lines is also illustrated within the concepts of this card, as can be seen in the diagrams used by acupuncturists, together with the chakras and the need to balance the energy flows through them. One can go on and on, but to give an example of this card in use - should one find the Star card appearing prior to the Never and Body cards it can indicate that you should meditate on the energies in the Universe by imagining a star radiating powerful light like the sun towards your body. The Never in this particular spread indicated to me that you cannot alone expect a planetary change - time - to alter your bodily strength.

7. THE HOME

A very full picture of a cosy country home in subtle colours which invite you to enter. The crisp white table cloth enhances the cleanliness of the room as the table is laid for tea. The reds of the fireplace and regency stripe wallpaper bring forward the feelings of love and warmth together with the interpretation of generosity. Whereas the general browns of the card give the meaning within the concepts of colour awareness, of practical protection, then the blues of the plates and rug represent the peaceful healing states.

"Home is where the heart is" and never more so than with this card which represents the trusted simple things in our lives that we sometimes undervalue. We all need the security of a comforting environment yet one must not forget that the home can be the person themselves; not just where they lay their head down. We are also what our background has made us. Naturally, this card can be interpreted simply as someone's home; just what the person is missing or has lost or then again left behind!

One has to remember when reading this book that in most cases when a 'reading' is required the Querent is not happy and there is something wrong in their life, so the happiest meaning of the card(s) is often left to the picture(s). Thus, the mugs can be an indication that the Querent is lonely and in need of company around the home. The blazing fire can bring memories forward from childhood such as homemade bread, toasted in front of an open fire which may be interpreted - depending upon other cards present - as someone living in the past or simply reminiscing to find one's roots. We may also draw upon the definition of a psychological need to get away from the confines of a home which is too traditional and thereby suffocating.

If you have opened your intuitive side to the degree of properly linking with the other dimensions of life (see chapters on Meditation and Psychic Development) this card may draw forward, when in layout with the Death card, links from the other side of life. Yet in a layout showing the Cave, Beast, Home and Liberation respectively the signals imply an unhappy childhood from which one is escaping.

A particularly good technique in meditating with this card is to allow your eyes to blur and drift towards the open fire and see what you may see!

8. WORK

This is a very simple card just showing cogs and wheels joined together with rods and chains, yet there is one small wheel with a cutting edge separated from the rest. Here within the concepts of colour awareness, are the colours of materiality, depression, and practicality with selfishness.

There are so many facets of life where the word Work can be applied yet so many times we have to sit back and let the wheels and cogs of the world move at an infinitely slow pace. One has to realise that all aspects of your life affect someone else - ultimately movement at the other side of the world affects you eventually - so from the outer limits of creation to the inner most points, movement is in play at all times.

Initially the picture in front of you may make you think of machinery and the complexity of factories. The card itself is symbolic of our working lives, firstly our jobs and then of our place in the economic world.

Naturally, the thought of work may be depressing or exciting in itself, but the necessity to work is there in this day and age so the card represents the materialistic aspects of life. However, as you allow your intuitive instinct to prevail, many other angles will slide in front of your mind's eye from working in groups, as in a team, to the loneliness working in isolation as a writer.

To everyone, there is a time in life when the word work and it's variety of associations becomes relevant, from the richest of men and women delegating arrangements for their finances, to the poorest worrying about where the next meal will come from and whether they will simply ever work again. A mother works at bringing up her children, and in the home she works at many different jobs from nursing to being a financier. Children have to work at their lessons in school whether or not they are going into the business world or art. But as already suggested, your intuitive/psychic ability will assist you to draw on the more precise personal aspect of this card when it is within a spread.

For me, there have been times when the work card, together with the Sage, Voyage, Skills and Liberation cards, has given the Querent's job as being a

Bank employee who travelled around the country assisting the managers of Banks that were ceasing to trade!

Yet another time those very same cards gave me a Philosophical Teacher who travelled around a number of training groups passing on knowledge and assisting advocates to open their minds more effectively.

Another example of the involvement of the Work card in a spread was when the Sage was followed by the Father, Skills, Tree, and Work, and the interpretation was of a family business where the knowledge was passed down and the business was of watchmakers!

As you will already have realised, Psycards can be used at varying depths and hopefully the previous comments will assist you to see the ways in which this particular card may be used. Of course, it can simply imply that there is work on the way. The Work card followed Cave and Money would represent a person with a job that was somewhat depressing plus a low pay-packet. However, these cards in reverse order would suggest that to find the coins you would need to get out of the depressed state and get to work.

Drawing your attention to the small wheel at the top which is separate from the rest and has a cutting edge so different to the rest - perhaps indicative of a person ready to fight alone in a spiteful way.

9. THE SKILLS

The pictorial imagery and colours incorporated in this card are perfect for its title of Skills, a crossbow of light brown wood at the ready with arrows and a red quiver nearby. Here is the brown of practicality and the red of ambition, putting this together upon the beautiful green grass which within the colour awareness coding is versatility, you have vitality and alertness - all that are needed within Skills.

It is a card that can give many surprises, since we use skills in a variety of dimensions in life from the everyday work aspect into the self-realisation levels; from manual work to meditation; sporting prowess and the equipment we use.

There is a need for expertise and, as with talent, there is always the need to stretch oneself; to keep the bow in tip top condition in order to achieve that perfection, or as near as possible, each time an 'arrow' is used; the quiver is continually full proving that we can reach even further into ourselves.

The Skills card symbolises firstly the natural abilities we are born with, together with those that we acquire following education in different fields. Since Skill comes to the fore with hobbies such as art and sports, our adaptability is also represented in this card but, naturally, there can be the reverse and a need to acquire skills may be the full interpretation. However, since the bow is ever ready and the quiver full, both giving the appearance of alertness, the implications are ever to the fore that we can still find those reserves necessary to acquire the attributes to get us out of a difficult situation, which is implied in a card line up of Destruction, Beast, Cave, Skills, and Liberation.

There has been the odd occasion within my work when this card has correctly been interpreted purely as the Querent being involved in archery, then again, the fine wood carvings on the bow itself representing a gentleman engaged in woodwork and furniture restoration.

Obviously as you use the Psycards their own language develops and often takes you away entirely from the cards' actual titles. So it is with this card, in particular the sharp points of the arrows - although not seen, they can be felt

and then interpreted as 'arrows in the back', especially when in a layout progression such as Union, Destruction, Beast, Skills, Friendship, and Liberation. This combination refers to a deep friendship which has split, as has the river, under painful circumstances. One party is being vengeful in a backhanded way, so a friend is stabbing the Querent in the back, and the Querent should separate himself from the so-called friend.

10. MONEY

The rich earth ploughed into deep furrows together with the bare trees of winter; a farmer guides his horse-drawn plough, bringing forward a variety of brown shades which illustrate such varying characteristics as lack of imagination, depression, practicality and avarice. Under a grey white sky the light glints on coins showing through the turned earth, and within the colour consciousness interpretations this shading represents fear - which we often have when there is a lack of money!

"Money is the root of all evil", or so they say, but in this day and age it is a great necessity. How funny this card is - the money under the earth suggesting buried treasure, and the saying goes "As ye shall sow, so shall ye reap", yet one man's gain is sometimes another's loss. Then everything is of the Earth and so shall return to it!

The card looks barren, yet winter always does. But the seasons slip by, changes come, so keep your spirits up! 'Things never stay static' is one message incorporated in this card. Look at the furrows straight and deep, the good rich earth being turned in preparation of the regeneration to come and so should every chance in life. If one digs deep and long enough, the rewards eventually come to the surface.

Naturally, the initial interpretation for this card would be Money and its possible availability. From this you can develop the theme as to whether it will be (or was) achieved through work or luck; investment returns or inheritance. Always you must remember to become acquainted with the flow of the cards in groups to allow fuller and wider implications to be clarified. Other cards will also help you to decide as and when it will arrive, although the actual position of the card in a spread will solve a lot - such as past or future conditions.

Now as you drift from the title of the card into the picture fully, there will be thoughts of the farmers' long lonely hours of toil, which may be interpreted just as farming connections or then as a person who keeps going from dawn till late. There can be a general love of the countryside or a dislike of it due to mud and smells.

When the Money card comes up in a spread with the Home, Mother and Father, it may represent the farming connection even more so and bring thoughts of ancestors originating from the country areas.

Then again, should the Money card appear with the Warrior, Sage and Tree the symbology of the coins could be indicative of an antiques collector. However, in a layout with the Destruction and Cave cards the Money card may draw forward the interpretation of poverty and famine from disasters.

11. FRIENDSHIP

Rustic colours of a time gone by encourage you to join the revellers of this card inside the period alehouse. The men in their greys and browns typical of the era with silver buckles upon their black shoes. The colour of black in an aura would be interpreted as vice and malice, where silver in colour symbology would represent vivacity. Their lady is dressed in deep red, and this would symbolise sensuality, yet the dull green of the curtains and table cloth, which they lean upon, is calmness. How many times in circumstances similar to those pictured here do we need the calming influence around! Also, the delicate colours showing through the lattice work window encourage gentle peacefulness, healing the moods created within as the drinks flow freely.

Within the picture, we have companionship, friendship and relaxation with the hint of another about to enter the scene and join the party. There is also the gaiety of an exotic bird just waiting to copy the conversations as they often do.This is perhaps a subtle way of suggesting that one should be careful who hears your conversation, as it may be repeated to all and sundry.

Initially, a very happy card drawing your thoughts to your social life, good cheer, laughter and regular meeting places. Of course, as with all the cards it can be the reverse of what you actually see. Therefore, it is important to note the other cards around it, also to give your first impressions since it can imply that the card symbolises a situation lost and longing for its return. Then again, the Querent could be a person who detests social drinking or is even shy. To give you further assistance in 'reading' this card - and the others for that matter - just sit and ponder on its many associations before you start trying to do readings and thereby get acquainted with its language.

In the background, there are barrels of wines and spirits suggesting a party scene, or it may imply - especially if the Work card is adjacent - a working environment of a public house or licensed establishment.

If this card is in the position where you have chosen to express the nature of a person's character in a spread, then it generally bring forth thoughts of a friendly natured person - someone who likes to be out and about mixing with others, plus a good host(ess).

Unfortunately, it can also indicate that the person is sometimes too friendly or perhaps likes the "vino" a little too much; but who are we to criticise? We can only deem ourselves the position of giving the first impressions to the Querent that are given intuitively to us in a reading.

There has been the odd occasion when the positions of the feet and legs of the males and the hand of the seated male on the left, have brought forward the implication of bisexuality correctly, but then this closeness may imply brothers.

There are many times when the Friendship card has translated as difficulties within a relationship, such as in the following sequence - Union, Beast, Cave, Friendship, and this implies that there has been a breakdown in communication due to a disagreement. Of course, there can also be the interpretation in the following set of the inability to see who our real friends are, together with the loneliness of betrayal by those so-called friends - Friendship, Fool, Destruction, Liar, and Cave. Yet we all have the ability to choose, should we realise this. Add the final card of Liberation to this last sequence and you will find it interpreted to mean that you have chosen to move away from unsuitable persons!

We all have work friends, business partners and social friends as well as platonic relationships, and all are included in the symbology of this card.

Finally, it would be interesting to place oneself in a meditative state and use the picture as the imagery for the meditation exercise, to see perhaps who the new friend is, or perhaps the outcome of the threesome when the fourth person joins the picture!

12. FORTUNE

Varying shades of yellow bring this card to life. From the dark confines a spiralling staircase grows towards the garret where sits a wooden locker seemingly full of treasure, including what appears to be a chalice. But how deep is the treasure?

The dingy colours within the steps allow the interpretation of suspicion and false optimism, through to the higher soul qualities of the lighter yellows, to be illustrated. Perhaps this is indicative of the expression upon the face of our seeker climbing the stairs, which are obviously well worn from past explorers, since it looks as though he thinks we are competitors trying to reach the prize before he does. However, as many have tried the path before and still the treasure is there to be taken, he just needs the perseverance in balancing to keep climbing since there are no handrails for support and a seemingly bottomless pit of darkness into which he could fall. But where does he go when he reaches the top?

There can also be implications here of someone creating a storehouse of valuables for themselves from the well worn staircase, and a timely warning to be wary of the illusion of money - it is not everything.

Initially, though, the Fortune card is indicative of that upward swing in life's finances, together with one's aspirations and dreams of increased wealth. It represents the success achieved by good luck and persistence plus luxuries in life generally.

A delightful card to have appear on the future side of a spread due to its promise of goodies, but sometimes sad if drawn on the past side, since this can indicate the gains of the past now being lost. If you find the Fortune card in the centre of a spread indicative of the present, and the Stranger and Destruction following it, you will surely realise that it is a warning to be careful how you tread on that upward staircase of ambition, not to trip others on the way or push them over the side into the darkness.

Of course, this card also represents in other ways the fruits of life by way of the treasures of a personal nature, so if in a layout with the Sage and Message, it implies success in an academic field.

Yet a display showing the Cave, Friendship, Fortune and Peace would stand for a move away from depressions into a new friendship which would continue to grow into something special. However, in a spread designed to show spiritual progression, the Fortune card followed by Peace would simply confirm an upward path into the light.

ARCHETYPES

Here, under the title of the Archetypes, we have those prototype model qualities which reflect the underlying forces that have directed the elements of our psychological levels since primitive man. So, therefore, the archetypes are alive in us and constantly recurring around us.

There is the guiding FATHER quality together with the compassionate MOTHER instinct in everyone - we all have parents as well! In simplest terms, of course, there is also BIRTH and DEATH in all aspects of life - the beginning and end. Yet again, we all experience the sexual drives of the LIBIDO card at some point. Finally then, without the DESTRUCTION of PEACE how can we appreciate the actual PEACE itself?

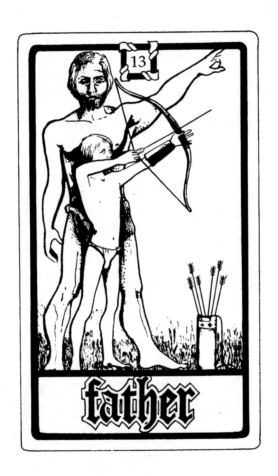

13. FATHER

A man stares out at us whilst directing his child in archery. Here, the clear red of the quiver and arm shield brings forward again the interpretation of ambition within the realms of colour consciousness. In the background, we have the light green of success, together with the pure ethereal and bright blues representing (respectively) devotion and sincere loyalty, all enhancing the qualities of a perfect father figure.

It is a card which gives purpose and force to action, symbolising the masculine element in the nature of each one of us, but one must remember that the symbology can also infer the parent/original part of the company or even the problem in question.

However, initially, the card does signify a father together with his authority, knowledge and strong protection. Sometimes, though, there appears to be a cautionary expression in the face of the Father, as his having been there before us perhaps means that he knows best and we should listen. Yet naturally it can stand for an older person to whom we should turn to for advice and guidance.

When the Father card is in a spread with the Body card, the indications may be read as a health problem concerning the older male. There are so many implications which can be attached to this card from the figurehead, thus from the "provider", to the launching pad of a project. The majority of us look to our parents for reliability and example. Of course, there are the occasions when these qualities are missing, but we all have memories of one sort or another to be illustrated in this card.

The Father card can also be defined as authority, power and discipline. Although you may have a loving docile father image in your mind, another may associate the word with thoughts of punishment, cruelty and sternness. Therefore, in a spread with Liberation, it implies a 'child' trying to break loose from a dominant or old-fashioned parents' direction. When in a layout with the Prison, Beast and Warrior, the explanation could be of restrictions, harsh discipline and a dictatorial manner.

Of course, there are always the occasions when the father figure actually represents a female and, therefore, the card enforces the archetypal avenue of thoughts initially as to the guiding influences in life. At first glance, this card gives me the sensation of being told to move forward in life and not backwards.

There are times when the Father card in a layout with Home, Fool, Beast and Liberation suggests that the Querent is being turned out of their home! However, in a spread with the Skills and Sage it may signify learning that may be received by an older male or through that gentleman.

Finally, the arrows are symbolic of the male organ and, therefore, lead into the following cards naturally.

14. MOTHER

Against a delicate background of blue and green a mother sits serene and protective, with her children in the sandy coloured, colonial style armchair reminiscent of India. Now, the sandy colour represents strong ideals of a practical nature suited to a mother image, whilst the chair's shape is also symbolic of the womb and ovaries and, therefore, receptive to the arrows of the previous card, whereby they then lead into the following card - Birth.

The son in this delightful picture appears to try and take up his father's role by standing close to the woman with a protective arm across both his mother and sister. The young girl sits restfully upon her mother while the baby gazes from behind the mother's back - obviously securely strapped. The apple-green of the adult's dress stands for sympathetic humanitarian ideals, whilst the turquoise of the childrens' clothes represents 'seeking maturity' (see colour interpretations).

This card may be representative of an actual mother or just a person - male or female - with compassionate tendencies towards others. Sometimes it shows a male's inner most tender heart towards an individual or mankind. It would also be indicative of a lady with an exceptionally compassionate heart for all children or mankind in general; then again she could be just possessive - as always, it asks you to allow your intuition to flow freely.

Although initially this card stands for the feminine, mothering side of nature; perhaps the Earth Goddess - we must remember the Yin and Yang principle in all, together with imbalances. This card can imply a person's need to be loved as a child, purely and simply for themselves and not for their possessions. But again there can be the need to break those apron strings from a parent or older woman who is possessive and smothering in their attention.

This particular card may draw your thoughts to fertility, especially if it is in a spread with the Birth card and, if there is the Cave and Liberation card, could imply the inability to have children. However, should the Mother and Birth cards be joined by the Peace, the implications could just be the physical birth expected.

Now, whilst looking at the little one peeping over the mother's shoulder, should the Birth, Death and Cave cards appear, the indications would possibly bring the inspired thoughts of a baby lost at birth.

Another variation on this theme would be the Mother card in a layout with the Liberation, Fool and Cave signifying a one-parent family. Allow your mind to flow, and when the Journey and Liberation cards appear with the Mother, you may find you are drawn to thoughts of India as I was at one time, due to the chair, and found that the interpretation was correct.

All the cards give much wider implications when they are seen in operational displays with others, therefore, examples have to be given.If you see the Mother next to the Beast, the Inquirer, Destruction and Cave the symbology would be of a generation gap with the problem of being unable to get close to the mother. Yet if it is laid with the Body, Destruction, Inquirer, Liberation and Cave, this would suggest pain and suffering in both parties due to illness and having to make arrangements for the elderly parent.

Finally, in a layout with the Peace, Sun and Fortune, the Mother card would lead to thoughts of a parent with an affectionate nature and full of generosity.

15. BIRTH

The richness of the green contrasting with the delicate blue sky brings thoughts of spring and summer which are enhanced within the pictorial imagery, of a new shoot bursting from its lush virgin fold and sparkling with dew.

This is a very good card to appear in a layout, as it is always a promise of movement which is following from a Universal Law. It gives growth in its more natural way whether it be of an actual life, situation or plan - it indicates the time has come to stop going round in circles and take decisions for the now. It is unstoppable - change must come as surely as day follows night, so the time before birth is the tunnel of death from the previous situation and you have come through it all ready to surge into new adventures.

This is the card of spring, the psychological growth with the promise of new beginnings, the metamorphosis of all. Obviously the first impressions displayed by this card are those of the birth itself - the new life, yet the transformation is often a sign of pain first (as there is with physical birth), then the freshness of the new awareness. There are also fairly clear suggestions of both male and female symbology in this image, bringing forward the theme from the Father and Mother cards, together with the Yin and Yang which is in us all.

Of course, there are many times in life when we are in situations where the circumstances seem impossible and we are as the chrysalis just waiting for hope. When this is the case and your reading shows the Prison, Birth and Liberation appearing respectively, the definition would be that the hope, at last, is a promise of possible change.

The more one accepts that change is imminent, the easier life can be. Therefore, when the Birth card is followed, perhaps with the Cave and Sun, the moment has come when one must go with the flow if you want to avoid pain and discord, growth of life into the light.

Now, when this card is in a line made up of Work, Cave, Destruction Birth and Skills, the implications would be of the beginning of a new phase such as a new job. Should you be looking for the revival of a relationship, then look for an arrangement of Union, Beast, Liberation Birth and Peace, but here you would also need to be asking the relevant question at the time of laying the cards of the total spread.

Naturally, the card can be taken to symbolise a variety of events. In a spread showing the Libido, Beast, Cave, Birth and Sun, the indications here would imply that the personality in question is a bit hasty at times, moody and needs to change their attitude into a more sunny disposition. However, a display of Peace, Tree, Scales, Birth and the Stars may lead to an interpretation of a religious nature, such as past knowledge being weighed up against a new thought leading to a new concept.

16. DEATH

The card every non-reader dreads to see in a spread, always fearing the worst, although, it is really more often a card to be welcomed - heralding the finish of one phase of life. However, the pictorial illustration is at night; under the faint glimmer of an unseen moon one sees an ancient burial mound, together with the skulls marking the entrance, depicted in the general colours of disease! The light grey of the pillars symbolises fear, that which you would feel at the beginning of an unknown tunnel such as this.

The reflected design of the entrance showing within draws you into the mysterious depths, whilst outside, the poppies show a promise of remembrance and a way forward as nature provides a new season; however, within the Auric colour concepts the dark and cloudy reds mean anger and cruelty, respectively. Now, the black within this card is heavy and brings forward the meanings of malice, vice and deprivation which, in turn, would make one depressed, and this mood is symbolised in the brownish-greys. All together, the colours shown here illustrate the lowest depths of man, but one must remember that this should also be a turning point to rise again and be reborn.

This can be a frightening card indicative of the biggest possible changes, even trauma, in life, and the poppies suggest that courage is needed. The Inquirer is led towards the opening and drawn further and further within, through the progressively darkening stages. Have courage to move forward; as the seasons die and pass, so is born a new day. A change is represented here within this card - as in all methods of divination, the stage of death is very important in our lives, such as the stepping stones through schooling, business and retirement.

The tunnel in this card with receding archways often emphasises a phase that we can sense around us but not wish to face up to. Now the poppies may bring another connotation, the memories of battlefields, wars, waste and carnage that comes before the final change in ages past but is always there amongst us in the world. However, the shadowy light in the picture can give a promise of understanding dawning. Also note how the shapes of the Birth and Death cards fit together.

Initially, then, you can see that this card represents the final change, the actual step which has taken you over the gateway into the new phase and it is death that makes you change!

The other implications of the Death card touch upon our psychological and emotional sides from the need to change attitudes when outlived modes of existence have to be revamped, thus the old self must die. Finding the Death card between the Libido and Birth cards within a spread may show us that at the end of a particular set of circumstances we need to let the old self die, thus give way to change.

The end of a difficult era in business matters can also be indicated by the Death card when it appears within a spread which has, of course, been laid specifically with the situation and business side of life in mind, i.e. Work, Beast, Destruction, Money, Stranger, Death, Birth and the Tree.

There are occasions when we need to make a sacrifice in order to assist our families into a new life and thereby finish a lingering situation. This may be seen within a layout giving the Mother, Father, Union, Cave, Destruction, Death and Liberation cards, from which the interpretation would read 'Parents trying to keep family together and guide them, but parents drifting apart due to depressions caused by devastating situations which need to be ended, so that all can go forward over the bridge to freedom from restrictions'.

Naturally, with the use of your inborn intuition, there will be occasions when, for example, Destruction, Cave, Never, Prison, Beast, Death and Liberation cards indicate a physical passing, but this should never be taken from face value alone. Your intuition and psychic sensitivity must draw you to the same conclusion for it to be given as an actual death.

I have also found that the Death card can imply that the Querent has some degree of clairvoyant ability and has actually seen a loved one who is in another dimension of life; a ghost, as some call persona without a physical body!

17. THE LIBIDO

Firstly, again I will deal with the colours and their interpretation within the card's design - here strong bold colours and action within the pictorial vision in this card define the strength of its character. Vivid greens of creativity carpet the ground whilst overhanging clusters of orange bring energy and vitality of spirit forward, enhancing the peacock as he displays his plumage.

In this card gushing waters tumble over rocks to froth up into white delight, symbolising purity and cosmic awareness, whereas the rich blue of the peacock represents forcefulness. All this together represents the various energy drives of nature in its lush splendour.

This card needs thought as to which portion you are drawn to first, to give you the correct interpretations and their many implications.

Libido - initially meaning the sexual drive, the life energy of the personality, is the emotional driving force behind all human impulses, simply - the desires. This card represents an awakening of the self and the greater awareness of life from experience, which will automatically happen as one grows older, through the interaction of various emotions created by the interplay with all those which we come in contact with. Incorporated in this particular card are a variety of symbols illustrating the various associations which the card may touch upon, and each facet needs to be drawn to the eye's attention.

The top half of this picture shows us a peacock in full proud display with water tumbling down a waterfall smoothing the surfaces of the rocks, from which an interpretation can be derived at implying a full awareness of self and the charisma of that knowledge! There are also the glorious shades of autumn to emphasise the knowledge which is there in the autumn of our lives together with the awareness of how fully pleasurable that life can be when you are experienced!

In the lower half of the card, you see the bird of comparison - the peacock with his plumage withdrawn together with a colourful snake and spring flowers to complete the image of inexperience, yet with the potential for blossoming. Thus there is a holding back, which all together implies innocence, the spring time of our lives being the birth of awakening from a child learning to crawl onto the first kiss. One should notice that the grass area close to the snake is overgrown, but cropped short on the other side, suggesting a snake in the grass! The need for caution when experimenting in unknown areas is the advice, and to be wary of hidden motives. However, a hint of blue water in the bottom right-hand corner gives nourishment even to the multi-coloured snake, thus encouraging one to continue. Of course, using the Eastern esoteric role gives a deeper meaning, symbolising the awakening of the kundalini in preparation for using the psychic forces being expanded.

However, since the peacock also uses its plumage to frighten off others less experienced, awareness of possible danger is implied as well. Sometimes, then, this card can indicate an over-sure person.

Should this card appear with Birth, Stars and Union, the definition would almost certainly be of an awakened sexual need, and if the Liberation card followed the progression could be towards a freedom of expression and action.

If the question is spiritual, and the order is Birth, Libido, Stars and Peace, you could conclude that new awareness had dawned on a high level and complete enlightenment of cosmic and spiritual peace was available. Yet if the line up was Libido, Friendship or Union, with Liar, Destruction and Liberation, it could mean that new knowledge within a relationship had been received, causing that connection to break down completely. However, if a layout showed the Liberation followed by the Sage, Libido and Skills, the definition would be of new hobbies achieved after study perhaps of an artistic value.

I must also add that when being consulted by a male, particularly youthful, and the Libido has appeared with the Father, Warrior and Liar, I have correctly interpreted it as homosexuality - there is always a tactful way of expressing this! The same has gone with females when the line up was the Beauty, Warrior, Liar, Libido and Mother. It must be emphasised, however, that your intuition must also lead you to this conclusion, since a few embarrassed faces may be seen if a mistake is made - it could be just that they prefer the friendship of their own sex.

18. DESTRUCTION

The wanton destruction of a holy war in full force shown here. What starts a war? A fight between tribes, nations and people? One often hears this cried! But then what starts a disagreement between man and woman, neighbours, families, friends? Do we ever stop and think of what we are saying before it starts? If you are clairvoyant you would see the reds of aggression tinged with black in another's aura, warning you of what might happen if you continue acting towards them in a specific way.

Cannot 'men' see that each is entitled to his own opinion, own life, own way of belief and existence - NO - we never stop until it is too late, and that is what you are shown within this card through its colours and pictorial display- the battle itself. Yet, again, if things were not destroyed how would you build new again, whether it be life, loves or buildings? When are we stretched most? When do we learn most? During and after the struggle, and it will always be the same, just as the farmer burns off the stubble to clean his land for new growth.

The picture itself shows a holy war, a scene of horror and carnage depicted with the castle being stormed by medieval soldiers, the differences of opinion and need for obliteration in the wake of newness being emphasised by the burning of the church in the rear of the scene.

This card symbolises a sudden unavoidable change which arrives through a shattering experience, sometimes pointing to being in the centre of a very unpleasant situation which is beyond one's control. See the woman tied to the stake, helpless, unable to free herself of havoc all around. Yet remember if you do not fight, you can be in the middle of chaos but untouched.

War, vandalism, wanton and futile destruction are, unfortunately, a part of human nature which does not change. This is reflected in many cultures and religions, for example in Indian mythology by the Goddess Kali. As it is an element of the collective psychology, there is a warning in this card of the fearful destructive side of our own nature and that of our fellow man.

Should this card follow the Peace card in a spread, the implications can be of a breakdown in beliefs, ideals and religious concepts. Yet if these two cards

are followed by the Yes and Tower cards it can be pointing to the need to fight for one's own personal truths through opposition.

There are also occasions when the Destruction card is indicative of a religious awakening due to a sudden revelation, especially if it is in a layout with the Liberation, Birth and Sage cards, respectively. However, when reversing the order of the last cards mentioned, the illustration would be of a person breaking away from religious traditions.

One must remember, again, that the actual positions of the cards in a spread must also be taken into account as to whether the condition is past, present or future. In a layout with the Now and Money cards, the thoughts and ideas related to the harvest stubble being burned down to make way so that new growth may come forward, thus you are being told there is a need to clean away the past rather harshly.

When you are doing a reading which is related to a relationship that is breaking down and the following cards appear in order - Union, Beauty, Warrior (or Mother and Father), Beast, Destruction and Liberation, the implications would be of a separation or breakdown due to the uncontrollable behaviour of the parties concerned, owing to the evil temper that raged into hatred of one person (the spread's actual position, meanings and the sex of the Querent would define which person was the guilty party).

There are times in life when we can sense the integration of different warring elements within our personality on a higher plane, and this can be signified in a layout which contains a card representing the self, plus the Stars, Libido, Beast, Destruction and Peace.

19. PEACE

The most beautiful card in the pack showing a pictorial description of that which we all crave for - the peace and tranquillity of oneness. Delicate and restful golden tones warm this card and bring forward the colour meanings of the higher soul qualities, but intermingled with the dull shades to represent false optimism. Also depicted here are the soft blue-greens which calm the restless mind and make it a perfect card for meditation. The great stained glass window, showing a healing mandala, is flooded with light which shines into a beautifully colonnaded cathedral. Obviously a cathedral which can be of the physical world or the etheric and astral planes.

A spiritual awareness and striving is often initially indicated by the appearance of this card, whereby thoughts flit to that need for tranquillity (see chapter on meditation). Therefore, sometimes it is indicative of a need to bring a quieter time into one's life and surroundings.

Look at the patterns throughout the card symbolising the pathways of life and how they interchange. The squared floor of this card's chamber is symbolic of the force of foundation needed in life, the pillars added strength to the structuring then the circle represents the original foundation force of creation, all of which relate to our total being and the requirement of balance.

To extend the interpretation of this card further, we need to place it amongst others and within a spread so that its own language may develop from its actual position.

When the Peace appears in a character analysis it gives the description of empathy, which the Inquirer/Querent gives to others. If the Peace card is followed by the Liar, Money and Libido, the explanation can be that the Querent has neglected their spiritual well-being and perhaps prayer is the call of the day.

Now, if the reading is questioning a health condition, a layout including a card to represent the patient is needed. Then the Body, Beast Scales and Peace would lead to the clarification of equilibrium, stability and a definite restoration to good health on the way, and if followed by the Sun - a period of convalescence would be an advantage.

This is a card implying initially spiritual wholeness but also sincerity and recuperation; therefore, it is an excellent card to appear in any line when you are searching your heart for a positive outcome.

Naturally if the question is regarding the development of a relationship and the cards which appear relate to that question, such as the Warrior, Beauty, Union, Libido, with the Peace appearing towards the end of the lay, then of course, it implies that a very good progression should be expected. However, if the relationship has been going on for some time and the Peace card appears in the past position, the suggestion would be that the best times have already been, and it perhaps needs rejuvenating.

SYMBOLS

The symbols are the cards which represent the signs that can be found in everything and are definitions of abstract ideas born in man's psyche.

Here, they are suggesting rather than depicting reality, symbolising themes in life and the unconscious, thereby assisting one to theorise the different aspects of situations. The Symbols are rich, powerful and ambivalent in all cultures, myths, poetry, picture stories and nursery rhymes, etc.

20. THE SUN

A card which gives me fully the feeling of being in the sun; children dancing joyfully around the fields under the sun's golden rays. Summer brightness and vitality spring forward from the colours of the card which is full of pictorial significance. The ripe yellow corn shows a time of fullness with the sheaves of wheat to give a time of thankful rejoicing yet the children still skip around their Maypole, in an ancient dance of spring fertility.

The sun stands for power and creative forces, it symbolises confidence with success together with a benign influence on all around. It also represents the conscious power of the intellect plus that unseen force behind the Universes.

The obvious suggestions of this card being a male symbol and the influence of masculine strength are illustrated by the dainty phallic symbol in the centre front, together with the traditional Maypole. However, this card when displayed in a layout with the Libido can give an indication of the opening awareness of one's own sexual side. Depending upon whether the Querent is a male or a female - the Sun and Libido together with the Beauty or Warrior can give expansion to this private area! The sheaves of wheat in the background hint of past associations, but the blue cornflowers amongst the unpicked wheat give a promise of more to come. The card in its totality is a promise of better times to come when in the position of present or future, but obviously as one learns to use the intuition of the mind it can be wishful prayers.

Children always give the essence of happiness and innocence, perhaps depicting the need for the Inquirer to cheer up or not be so trusting!

The face of the sun in this illustration is changeable; at times it is sad then naturally bringing forth thoughts of longings, yet the sun itself is uplifting and revitalising.

Should this card appear in a spread with either the Beauty or Warrior plus Libido, the implications could be extroversion, yet if the Fortune card is present the solution then implies that the extroversion would be of a generous nature, and not a selfish one.

There is a positive power and warmth within this card which is generally obvious in all its associations; however, this can be a past condition which is sought once again, providing the other cards and their positions imply the same.

The full impact of this can be seen in the following group of cards - the Union, Sun, Beast, Destruction and Liberation, where all the goodness appears to be in the past.

When in a reading which is appertaining to a health condition, the Sun has been known to represent purely sunlight, tonics and sunflower seeds! If the Sun card is found between the Sage and Stars we would, perhaps, be intuitively drawn to the intellectual mind and its power to learn and expand.

21. THE MOON

A brilliantly detailed Moon majestically radiates its mauvey aura out into the night's blue sky. Under the colour awareness themes, the dark blue symbolises spiritual questing whereas the mauve shows spiritual motives. Now the dark bluegreen of the sea below leads us to the interpretation of soul searching, from which a large crab climbs over rocks with its shell reminiscent of a cat's face.

The Moon is always given the symbology of illusion and the feminine aspects; however, the Psycard Moon gives off a strong aura which often appears to readers like a rainbow. This allows the interpretation to alter slightly into the feelings that the illusion had already lifted or is just being removed, since one is able to see all the layers; also, the feminine aspect here is really the intuitive self and not the physical.

The crab often draws your attention to the Cancerian traits, but always the card represents movement in some direction, as the ebb and flow of the tide is linked to the moon's waxing and waning. In some lights, where the crab takes on the look of the fat cat's face, there is a warning which can be that even a soft furry cat has sharp claws, so be alert. The large crab climbing over the rocks seems very strong with a tough, hard shell, implying self-preservation - yet there is a soft inner self, enhancing the illusion that some people, especially men, like to project in order to cover their sensitivity. The water has the look of deep oceans and is very indicative of the emotional levels, together with the need to look within deeply. There are times when we, ourselves, are just like barnacles - clinging - usually due to the depth of our emotions, so take warning from this and do some self-analysis in order to cleanse yourself.

The Moon also signifies our intuitive psychic self and, therefore, is an excellent image upon which to meditate. From this it can be deduced that the card also represents the unconscious self, the unconscious acts that at times we need to be made aware of. Although it is a card symbolic of change, you should remember that the healing process is also incorporated in change, but as well, we have here the card which stands for fickleness and falsity - this would be emphasised naturally in a spread with the Liar present.

When the Moon card is found in a layout together with the Libido and Stars your intuition may very well deem that the Querent has experienced psychic phenomena to one degree or another, and if these cards are followed by the Stranger and Friendship, the indications are that open discussion is needed to give clear understanding to the events.

If the Moon card is found in a display concerning work or a relationship, between the Cave and Liberation, the interpretation would be of the need to withdraw into oneself in order to reassess, and remove illusions prior to moving into a different pathway. There are times within a character reading when the Moon card, of course, gives the definition simply of a Cancerian personality. However, if it is found next to the Fool, the correct description may be of a person who spends most of their time with their minds in the sphere of illusions, such as a daydreamer, or one who is simply not interested in the material world.

In a spread leaning towards a working aspect, I have found that when the Moon follows the Voyage, Skills and Message, the deduction was of a night fisherman! However, on another occasion concerning the Querent's working life there was a line up showing the Sage, Skills, Stars, Tree, Moon and Stranger, illustrating a person involved in the craft of Moon Magic.

Should you find the following group in a spread which is relating to aspects of the Querent's personality, the indications would strongly illustrate someone who is deeply depressed and needs help - Stranger, Cave, Moon and Never, since it implies that they cannot find their own way out of it.

22. THE STARS

Here we have the patterns of the "Aspects" from an astrologic chart super-imposed on the star-studded mystery of a night sky. Amongst the pinky-mauve depth of the sky the three pathways are marked out in different colours - the black line perhaps representing us with the heavy material life style; whereas the blue pathway would represent the spiritual karmic path and the pink lines symbolically standing for an affectionate family tradition. The colour interpretation for the pinky-mauve sky is the awareness of an emotional yet spiritual, cosmic consciousness.

This card opens questions as to which path one might be on - which path to take? Then again, it asks if we are aware of the cycles of the planets/stars, the Id*, and how they effectively change our lives and influence our moods. The Stars brings forward in symbology the beginning of a new cycle of life, whichever way you care to look at it; the time when one phase has moved away and when we need just to have faith since these changes are beyond anyone's control. They are like the cosmic repercussions of evolution within every fibre of your being, those irreversible processes that change you from baby to the aged being.

Obviously, the position of the Stars card in a layout is extremely important, since this will indicate whether the cycle(s) are for the better or not. You may even find your eyes only being pulled to the brightest star shining through the darkness, inspiring the explanation that it is just the dawn of the changes.

As the saying goes - 'straight off the top of the card' - here is the card which represents the astrological and astronomical fields together with the everlasting side of our natures.

However, we need to be wary of the 'wishful thinking' aspects together with the experience of 'pie in the sky' ideas, and these thoughts can be emphasised if the Stars are followed by the Warrior and Destruction, since these together would imply a person who has grand ideas which usually crash. Thus the Querent needs to think logically and plan his/her pathways.

I have found that this card can bring to mind a variety of occupations and, if shown with the Skills and Work cards, has implied cartography (i.e.

roadways of the skies). Yet when the Voyage card appears as well it has drawn out the professions associated with airlines, from air hostesses to mechanics and flight controllers. This card also symbolises our deepest aspirations, the goals we set for the heights of intellectual and artistic achievements. I have always found this card signalling good times.

(*Id - the impersonal mass of interacting energies and forces constituting the unconscious of the Universe.)

23. THE TREE

Throughout the ages of Man, the tree has had many representations and associations. Here again it symbolises the various facets of life, wisdom and knowledge, yet the quantity of red used in the background of this card significantly illustrates the strength of vital energy, which is needed to force action into its growth.

The Tree of Life takes its knocks over the years of our existence, and there are many times when we need to lop off a branch or two in order to channel our energies more effectively, allowing the roots of our being to dig deeper, pushing ever more branches up to the Light.

Seasons come and seasons go, but the tree continues to give forth its annual dressing of leaves, each leaf being a thought, each branch and twig being a lesson in life, therefore, the whole tree symbolising knowledge whether learnt or yet to be experienced. Growth is there for all to achieve and strive for in whatever aspect you are interested in or referring to. For more about the Tree of Life concept within philosophy etc., one should refer to the world of books concerning the Qabalah.

This card is also symbolic of that which is in us all, the ability to find some knowledge within to help another soul along the pathway if one digs deep enough. The Tree card also stands for tradition, whether it is in a country, group of people or family, the roots deep in the soil - the past, giving strength to future links.

To give an example of thoughts that this card can produce, picture it between the Friendship, Skills, Sage and Message. Here there could be the construction of a group of people drawn together to use their abilities and the need to set up a traditional constitution in a formal way so as to assist the future membership in their understanding of its concepts. Then again, see the Tree in the following line-up - Union, Beauty, Warrior, Beast, Tree, Mother and Father. Now the interpretation would be of a young couple who are finding it hard to blend their relationship, being advised to turn to traditional methods and advice from the strength of parents.

In a spread when the Tree is displayed with the Skills, Sage and Work, you may find you are inspired to talk about a person's ability to teach others and pass on their knowledge in a formal manner, such as within the teaching profession, although if the Body card is present, the leanings could be more to the medically aligned professions.

The Tree card can draw you to nature and gardening concepts, particularly if in a layout with the Sun and/or Money cards - just look at their pictures and see the connections. Yet a reading that links just the Body and Tree cards together could bring forward the inspiration of energy lines such as meridians or leylines, with the roots and branches of the tree spreading out the energy in varying directions. Of course, there is the need to remember that the reverse is true - the need to grow, to uproot or prune - the requirement of stability, but without stagnation! Plus the symbology of the Tree of Truth, of course; these negative traits would require the additional negative cards to appear within the spread in appropriate positions to allow you to draw these conclusions.

24. THE SCALES

The deep shade of green within this card, if seen in an aura, would represent lack of self-confidence and, therefore, is well suited to a card symbolising our struggles to achieve balance, when so many times we actually need more confidence. The imbalance illustrated by the Scales is again reflected in the uncertainty as to whether the branch upon which they hang is strong enough to hold the weight of the unequal load of fruit. Then in the incompatibility of the species of tree and the incongruous fruit. Yet, all in all, the complete pictorial illustration is a perfect representation of what the card is intended to symbolise.

We can have here the Scales of Justice or the scales of Libra. We all need to weigh things up in life, and then there are the occasions when balance is needed. Noting that the tree is full of ripe fruit, which is ready to be weighed and used, together with the age of the tree shown in its twisted trunk, this card gives the need to balance and weigh up the knowledge/fruits of life which the ages have provided.

Naturally, the scales of justice have been known to weigh against us, so there are the times when we need to weigh life's pros and cons very carefully in order to bring balance into our inner souls.

The colours give a lush growth to the grass and some of the fruit has fallen thus showing perhaps, that there was a time when we have given bad judgement, but if we look to nature, there can be a softening to the fall. Although the greenery of the tree looks like a fir tree, the fruit could be taken as apples or even oranges, therefore, ensuring that we look at things carefully and not always take them at first sight.

There is also a suggestion from the fruit and its position, that you should never worry about the windfalls of life (what has gone): it is what is in the scales and/or on the tree (the present and what is to come) that are important.

Also hinted at here, are moderation and prudence in the affairs of life. There is a need to use common-sense in all areas, to create harmony and see the equilibrium and accord within the world of nature; to be at total peace we have to blend with nature.

I have found that when the Scales card appears after the Body and Cave, it simply means the Querent requires more fruit in the diet!

Should the Scales card appear with Work, Skills, Destruction and Friendship, your intuition would draw the conclusion that there needed to be more moderation in the chatter between work mates, otherwise they could be destroying their own dexterity.

However, when the Scales appear together with the Beast, Sage, Prison or Liberation, the leanings would naturally be towards the legalities of life, suggesting that a Judge could be presiding over a legal matter. Of course, if the Beast card was laying in the 'present' position and the rest in the future, this could all be taken as a warning to use temperance.

There are occasions when the Scales are used to bring to the surface the need for a person to be prudent in their endeavours, especially when it follows the card which is used as the Significator, representing themselves, and is in turn followed by the Tower, Destruction and Liberation.

However, the Scales card can also simply mean instability, in which case you would require other cards to give you the indications as to whether this referred to their state of mind, body or life style, although in most cases I have found that this card has appeared just as the Querent has realised that there is imbalance.

25. THE TOWER

Clean and simple lines bring us to a card which can be associated with so many facets of life, there being a great deal of strength in its design. A Castle tower on a hill, showing a beautiful blue sky and clear green grass (see colour interpretations, page129). A small point to note since I am trying to draw your attention to every facet of the Psycards, is that within the actual colouring of the Tower card, the blue sky has a deeper patch to the left of the Castle which can simply be used as the definition of a cloud over your dreams!

Many, knowing the Tarot and seeing the word "tower", expect the tower of the Tarot but, no, this Tower is very different, it is one which is proud, stern and unyielding.

This can be the mystical castle which we have built in our dreams, but when we go within, it may be quite different. The many windows give a hint of the variety of rooms and draw you into the mystery behind the Tower's bold facade together with its apparent lack of ground level entry; thus suggesting the hidden corners of our innermost illusions.

Initially, however, the interpretation of this card is strength - inner or outer - although other cards present may imply that it is the strength we need to find.

This card maybe used to indicate a physical building in comparison to the Home card, and actually when it appears with the Home card often implies a new home! Yet, when in a layout with the Work and Skills cards, it can just signify a large office building, and if the Sage is present could indicate an architect. However, if the Tower is in a spread with the Sage, Skills and Body, it has been known to indicate a hospital.

Often the Tower represents the super-ego which drives us to high ideals and challenges, but I believe you would require the Peace and Stars to be present as well in order to give this definition. Of course, on a lower level, it can also illustrate the enlarged ego and arrogance. Sometimes, when lying in a spread with the Beauty and Libido, the Tower can therefore indicate someone who is thinking too highly of themselves.

The Tower itself appears very sturdy in this picture, and occasionally gives the impression of a phallic symbol, but as this is generally a masculine card the inference is acceptable.

Yet delicate implications can also be brought up by this card, and there have been several occasions, when in a layout with the Warrior and Libido, that the interpretation has been of homosexuality (since in this day and age this factor is widespread, the need is there to understand its recognition within divinatory methods, and not to be shied away from). However, on another occasion, the Tower with the Beauty, Libido and Warrior has subtly implied a need to prove oneself as a male.

Naturally, there are the times when we build a wall around our hearts and emotions, thus this card is also symbolic of the invisible wall.

26. THE WHEEL

The pretty Dutch brickwork helps to bring interesting features to this card of gentle movement, although the light grey represents fear - perhaps fear of the unknown! There can also be a warning from the colours of the reeds - olive green; hints of possible treachery; yet the glint of the gold from the fish symbolises pure sincerity within colour concepts. Of course, the wheel pulses movement through all as water drips from the blades.

At times we feel that everything is at a stand still around us, and this card is initially indicative of a change in this phase of life - or the need to implement the change.

Another view of the card, the wheel of eternal life perhaps, is looking at the spokes of the wheel as the many facets of ourselves with those around us, and the connecting circular band the force which join us all together.

The reeds depict some of the tangle we manage to get into which stops the flow of the river of our life, and the wall, that inevitable brick wall that so many of us build around ourselves after disappointments and pain. However, the hint of gold from the fish near the reeds is a suggestion of better things to come should we look beneath the surface.

We also may elucidate spiritually with the Wheel - the centre being the beginning the spokes as the pathways in various lives whereby we move to the other circle and blades. Thus, we are able to leave these domains to go elsewhere.

Initially, a card of change wherever it falls in a spread, such as, Cave, Work, Wheel, Skills, Liberation and Sun; here the interpretation would be of depression due to a work condition being changed by an alteration of skills, leading to a feeling of freedom and light-heartedness. Then, when the Wheel is displayed between the Home and Tower, it simply means a change of home.

If the Wheel is shown following the Friendship and Liar cards, you may well find yourself elucidating upon the fact that there are so few friendships around of real sincerity.

Also, when you have a group of cards like Friendship, Liar, Beast, Never, and Wheel you could well be receiving a warning as to unseen treachery afoot and need to sift amongst the reeds to find the truth.

Yet a line up displaying the Cave, Wheel, Now, Stranger and Friendship might be telling you that it was about time you overcame your fear of strangers and dropped the barriers so that friendship could grow.

To show alternatives that the wheel card can produce, I give a little story: I was doing a reading for an unassuming gentleman who owns a large psychic bookshop and the following cards appeared - Stars, Sage, Wheel, Peace and Stranger, from which I deduced that he had found a new pathway of personal study- Buddhism - which was his peace, but that he shunned openly showing it to all.

CHARACTERS

All of life is a play, and we are the actors who perform the various roles by taking on the Characteristics of different personalities throughout the dramas of life.

The many facets of our personalities are depicted within these cards such as our tempers in the BEAST, innocence in the FOOL and deception in the LIAR. Then again the male or female can reflect the WARRIOR spirit or gentle qualities of the BEAUTY. Of course, we can be a Stranger to ourselves in certain circumstances or to our nearest and dearest.

Finally, we often have to become the SAGE to sort out problems in life.

27. THE BEAUTY

Exquisite details, such as the reflections in the leaded light window, bring this card to life and draw you into the elegant setting in which the lady walks. Her handsome crimson Tudor gown echoes within its colour the interpretation of sensuality, which the lady obviously radiates from her being, yet this is toned down by the soft blue of the inner sleeves and underskirt, thus bringing forward the symbolism of devotion.

What comes to mind first? Perhaps the fairytale "Beauty and the Beast"? Well, life does have its fairy tales if we don't look into its many facets clearly.

This card gives many little points to bring forward, starting with the beauty herself. The lady is continually looking at the window with its various lights, perhaps indicating a backward look on life?

Of course, you may feel she is looking at herself in vanity, or trying to re-appraise her looks with an eye to detail. We all like to look good at times, but on many occasions there is a necessity to look underneath the outer facade of those we meet. The gown shows a texture and may indicate a sensitivity to touch, but a person wearing this colour surely does not intend to be invisible. Perhaps we have here a lady who feels she is too much of an introvert and is, therefore, trying to change her image. This certainly appears the case when the Beauty card appears in a lay together with the Libido and Liberation.

Yet, of course, we need also to be aware of the other type of lady who is fully aware of her desirability and may have a habit of flaunting it to all, thus earning herself the title of a harlot, when reading the cards for a male Querent upon the question of a new love, the Beauty can represent the virtuous, ideal woman, full of goodness and fidelity. This card links to romantic desirability, hence also signifying true love.

When the Beauty is found in a spread such as the Tower, Skills, Beauty, Warrior and Stars, the implications would be that the female in question fitted the bill of a heroine of old, since she has strength of character, adaptability, sensitivity, courage and the tenacity to reach high goals. Naturally, your intuition may bring forward this interpretation, but slightly changed to indicate that the lady in question believes all these things about herself and actually thinks herself too important to all and sundry; then there would be a need to lay more cards to see if a fall was likely.

Still with the beauty herself, look to her gown; this may give you the impression of velvet with thoughts of a needlewoman, which may well be implied if the Skills card is present. Add to this image the patterns formed in the window, and you could be drawn to giving specifics, such as quilting, which in turn follows on to upholstery, antiques and interior designing, etc.

The gown itself lends texture to the picture, and this may simply indicate that the Querent has a sensitivity of touch, especially if the Body card is present, leading you to indications of a healing ability. Now with this same train of thought, if the Tree and Libido are also in the spread, the four cards illustrate a lady with an awareness of other peoples' needs in a caring way. However, should the Beast make a fifth card, the interpretation may imply that, due to her continual awareness of the delicate conditions of others, she has been overdoing it and has thus misused her own body, whereby she needs to be more sensitive to her own needs.

If we now allow our eyes to look to the rest of the picture, we see the garden which appears, from the reflections in the window, to be a walled enclosure, illustrating a person who keeps to themselves and only on their own terms allows others to draw close. The neatly laid garden with its leafy greenery gives the definition of precision and herbal knowledge. Often I have found that this card beings forward the intuitive links with loved ones who have passed from this dimension, especially those who had the qualities defined in the pictorial description and their surroundings when in the earthly life, such as the very neatly laid garden.

Finally, in a layout with the Birth, I have found that the Beauty has been indicative of a pregnant lady - a look to the illusion of the full hips. So let the patterns and shapes within the cards speak to you also.

28. THE WARRIOR

A card of strength and determination, stemming from the figure and the colours of the shields, which are mirrored in the flags and tents - the red of ambition together with the yellow of intellectual power.

There is, of course, a softening effect brought about by the delicate shades of the background countryside. Who is not a warrior sometimes, when faced with a need for strength against all odds? Initially, this card stands for the hero - the knight in shining armour - who rescues his princess from a fate worse than death.

As with the Beauty card, there is much to elucidate upon in the pictorial display, so let us first look at the gentleman, as I will call him for now. He is shown as a man of strength and purpose with a face that can be young or old, sad or smiling - depending upon how your eyes glance, thus the connotations depend upon your intuition at the time of the reading. Obviously, he represents that ancient ideal of medieval chivalry and the noble cause, but of course there is always the opposite. The male in question may need to be more chivalrous, or stand up for what he knows is right. The Warrior's face shows strain and this could have been brought about by his "Achilles heel" being damaged, therefore indicating a weak spot where strong armour may be broken into. Obviously, if the Querent is the gentleman in question, he may be warned to watch his weak spot, or actually take off the armour.

Our Warrior here is also the embodiment of masculine virtue and can represent the Sir Lancelot of your dreams, but the other aspect, seen in the construction of reversed crosses, is that often the 'knights' in real life end up showing their undersides which are all too often vengeful, quarrelsome and aggressive, giving you the male chauvinist...

The sword is drawn, yet in a resting position, indicating a battle won without blood-letting. The flags flying around the encampment show preparations for the celebration.

Although this card is usually representative of a male, it can also depict a female with a fighting or crusading spirit - remember Joan D'Arc. The Warrior may also signify a Querent who has ideals which are too high and, if

laid with Destruction and Libido, would indicate the shock of self-realisation dawning soon.

I have found, therefore, that this card floats from male to female, but it does vary also in a slightly different way in layouts concerning relationships, i.e. when the Father card represents the husband or older male, the Warrior may herald a newcomer to the scene or just a younger male acquaintance. There are those gentlemen who stay as protective friends throughout one's life, accepted by all as a true friend whatever sex they may be. These are also symbolised by the Warrior card.

Other connections include the battles we all have to fight in life, and enemies or hostile situations to be overcome; also military associations.

When the Querent is asking for guidance in a situation concerning offspring, together with the Father or Mother card (representing the Querent), Peace, Destruction, Beast, Mother, Tower and Wheel, the Warrior would imply that the parent needs firmness and severity to control the offspring and the situation would change.

Should the Warrior card appear in a spread with the Cave, Beast and Stranger, the suggestion would be an aggressive person around who can be rather fierce when opposed. Another symbolic suggestion (note the background of soft and distant features, yet the rough ground beneath the feet, suggesting gentle thoughts of the past in comparison to the harsh realities of the present) is often brought forward when the Warrior is followed by the Beast and Libido cards, showing it is not always good to be headstrong in struggles; often the gentler approach to problems is more effective in the long run.

The sword can also be symbolic of aggression, or a vindictive nature. It may be found that a Querent is being warned of a male acquaintance who perversely 'puts the knife in', or if the Beauty card is present, a female with a 'cutting edge to her tongue'. With the Peace and Destruction cards, the Warrior may indicate a puritanical religious leaning - note the crosses together with the sword. The Warrior can also bring forward the recognition of the Archangel Michael and, therefore, the need for protection on a spiritual level, especially when this card is with Peace, the Beast and Stranger.

29. THE LIAR

Here we have a card of questioning patterns and concepts with our jester to help you to question the validity of many facets of life and people. There is the dark cloudy red of his clothes, which symbolises greed in colour concepts and the dark olive green implying treachery both adding to the total warning of caution within the card. The shades used are those of the lower elements and chakras, yet the curtain of blue suggests an entrance through to the higher mysteries.

Obviously, the first implications of this card are those of deception, untruths and hidden motives, yet all of this can either be within yourself or from another. There is the need to observe the actual facets in the designs to define the symbology included in its perception.

The court jester is holding a mask, also a replica of himself, perhaps denoting that the mask is what is shown to the world, yet his true self is held in high esteem away from prying eyes. Therefore, your intuition could lead you to the interpretation of one hiding behind a false face advising the Querent to have caution, or the Querent themselves needing to put on a brave face and look at life through different eyes. Then again, they may need to remove the mask they are using and be honest with others. This latter interpretation would come to light in a spread with the Liar sitting after the card representing the Querent and following the Union, and two cards signifying the two rivals in the relationship being questioned, since we can be deliberately deceiving others.

Note the bells on the jester's clothes - is he trying to ring a few notes of awareness or conscience within his jesting? We surely all know someone who is cynical in their conversation or sarcastic in their comments, so here we have the warning of their presence in a specific situation.

Now, looking at the smiling mask, one wonders how many of our acquaintances are really smiling or laughing at us (just note the subtle difference). One can be with genuineness and the other insincerity. Your psychic awareness will lead you to the correct interpretation at the time of a reading but remember to use your first intuitive thoughts not those mulled around for several minutes as this will just confuse you.

Is the jester dancing on one foot or does your sight confuse you into seeing him balancing on a thin line, thereby lending the symbology walking a tightrope!

Since the chequered floor beneath his feet represents the fine line of balance required in life, here we are given the necessity to recognize the need for a balanced foundation in our values.

In the background there is a staircase leading upwards with the wooden panelled well underneath having a curtained area adding mystery, and notice the shadowy implications of someone hidden behind the curtain.

The runs of the staircase often give the feel of someone wanting to climb a ladder out of the pit of misunderstanding into another level of hidden truth.

Occasionally in a spread with the Money card there can be an indication of the need to tighten the purse strings brought about by the discarded drawstring purse.

When the Liar is laid in a spread together with the Libido there is often the suggestion that the Querent needs to look within himself to find a realisation of their own true nature.

Now if the Querent is seeking advice as to a relationship and the Liar arrives in the spread after the card representing the other party then it symbolises a person who keeps the truth to himself and is deluding the Querent. Of course, in a question relating to business deals the presence of the Liar would naturally indicate the possibility of a trickster and cheat present.

30. THE STRANGER

It is often with trepidation that we face strangers and that is well depicted within the colours of this card, yet there appears to be a brightness awaiting if you look for it. All of the dull and dark colours symbolise the worst aspects, therefore, the dark blue, red and green of our stranger's clothes increases the apprehension this person portrays. Add to this the dark brown behind the figure, bringing a warning of the need for caution - who would not be cautious of a Stranger walking through a doorway wearing a glove the size of this person's!

This gauntleted stranger standing halfway through the doorway has an androgynous face which adds to the mysterious unknown which the card symbolises.

The Stranger card represents a part of our nature shut away from view which is seeking entrance into our lives in a surprising way. We have here also an illustration of the anima/animus, that part of our psyche which is excluded, yet still there. There comes the time of life when we are shocked by events around us, into looking more fully at the Stranger within ourselves. How many of us also believe we truly know our nearest and dearest only to find a time when they are a complete stranger to us. Of course, we may also find that our parents are strangers, as indicated in a layout which includes either the Mother or Father card, Moon and Stranger.

Often the Stranger card is one stressing prudence and subtlety when meeting someone new or entering a new situation until fully in the light. New situations, of course, should always be looked into fully; however, there are occasions when the Stranger card tells one to look at a present situation as an outsider would to discern one's real position. This can be seen from a line-up of the Work, Beast, Cave, Stranger, Birth and Libido when trying to decide what is the pressure in a working condition.

Naturally, many read the cards to solve the question of what might be arriving in the future months, and here we have a card which augurs a warning since a spread showing the Stars, Cave, Stranger and Destruction would seem to imply unpleasantness in the future, together with feelings of uncertainty and apprehension before a downfall.

97

When the Querent is seeking guidance over a new friendship, the Stranger may symbolise a vagabond or gypsy-like nature.

Or, your intuition may reveal to you a person whose life has been far from pleasant and has led them to be an introvert. The subtleties of the gloved hand may lead you to conclude you need to wear kid gloves, especially in a spread showing a line-up of the Beast, Peace and Stranger. Yet in a display of the Warrior, Beast and Stranger it could represent the need to use boxing gloves!

Always there seems to be an unknown quality and uncertainty linked to this card. Since not all life can be pleasant, this card can also signify a period of time approaching when you feel left out of things and unable to move forward through the door and into the light.

31. THE SAGE

A fascinating card which can hold you spellbound, just as Merlin would. Although the dark colours of this aged gentleman's outer robe might make one wary of approaching him, this is softened by the shades of his sleeves and cowl. All around our Sage are the colours of secure wisdom and vitality of thought (i.e. the gentle soft browns and clear reds), glasses put aside and wisdom flowing, which rides above material needs. Shown here also are the natural shades of wood giving a restful atmosphere, but the energy that is needed to continually pull knowledge forward is given in the particularly clear red of the cloth furnishings.

The sage is the card of the professionals and wisdom on a variety of levels; therefore it also symbolises Truth, learning, sciences and general studies. There is a paradigm of ideas within the card in order to draw your intuition to the true interpretations relevant to the Querent's situation.

Firstly, look at the shelves, the collection of aged leather volumes hinting at knowledge - should the Body be present in your spread, letting one's eyes drop to the glass containers may bring thoughts of a Doctor and a consultation to mind. Yet if your attention is drawn to the books and scales at the same time, and in your layout the Prison and Scales cards are closeby, one might conclude the necessity to consult solicitors judges or the Law. The books and ornaments could also bring thoughts of an antique collector, especially if the Friendship or Beauty cards are close, since they also link with antiques; but I have, on occasion, simply found that the interpretation simply pointed to a collector of ornamental glass! So try not to always dig so deeply.

A layout showing the Sage present with the Body, Beauty, Libido and Skills could imply a herbalist with great knowledge, since thoughts come forward of the jars being full of potions and herbal concoctions.

Often, this card infers that a person with official standing is around or should be consulted, especially in a layout with the Message, Skills and Scales.

A display showing a line up of the Home, Tower and Sage could often represent estate agents involved, but if the skills card is also present, it can also stand for architects, together with plans drawn up, thus indicating his explanations may need to be referred to.

Naturally, within the theme of knowledge, the sage signifies a variety of links, and once again requires further cards to define its individual solution for the specific case in question. The Sage can represent a professor or teacher to whom the Querent should turn in order to expand their own knowledge, and this would be shown in a layout with the Skills, Father, Message and Liberation cards, since knowledge liberates the soul.

However, the eternal student is also implied by this card: thus a course of training can be indicated. Should the Body be present, it could be as a healer; Work could indicate scientific leanings, perhaps. The Stars may then imply an alchemist or astrologer.

The list is endless, and the card so comprehensive as to draw one's intuition to the fullest, thus even to the mystical and magical side with the wisdom of the archives - our Sage has been called a Guru, a Druid and the Merlin force. Link it in a spread with the Peace card and we can have the spiritual leaders and prophets. Bring in the Stars, Tree and Libido and you could get associations with the ancient laws and Merlin again. Therefore, the card can appear in a display when it signifies the need for deep thought and the going over of past experiences, knowledge and information. So we also find an explanation here of the necessity to use vision, sanity and the intellectual self.

Conversely, the Sage can symbolise the misuse of power and false prophecy, which is illustrated when it is between the Beast and Destruction. Here again, if the Libido is drawn with these cards, we can deduce that the person in question is suffering from self- deception within their misuse of the power. Look to the pyramid on top of the writing desk indicating ancient knowledge from distant shores, link the feather to the pyramid and scales, progressively leaning towards the Egyptian temple of Maat and the goddess of Justice.

This card is obviously an ideal one upon which to meditate, with many topics to use on your journey.

32. THE FOOL

A carefree mood spills out of this card, perhaps to draw you into a sense of a light-hearted outer display to cover a very nervous disposition, that which is often portrayed by the word and colour yellow. This card often makes me think of the 'Pied Piper of Hamlyn" - a fool to look at but not in reality. We also have within this pictorial theme a yellowy-green which represents, in colour awareness, the daydreamer. Yet the sharp blue of the sky symbolises a spiritual purpose, and perhaps this is depicted in the movement of the figure away from his material status - the building.

In mystical terms, the Fool is often the portrayal of a person aiming to lead their own way in life, often at the expense of others and also, on occasions, craftily. Therefore, we can sometimes have here indications which point to a person with a twist to their personality, such as the simple innocent looks which lead us to trust, whilst below the surface they have the determination to play their own tune in life. Thus, in a spread where the Beast is laid with the Fool, it is indicative of a carefree person with an obstinate streak determined to have the last word.

The Fool on its own in a layout concerning the Querent's personality may simply signify that they act quite differently when away from home, or they like to play the Fool! Yet again, if the Tree precedes the Fool and Libido, you maybe led to interpret it as a person with the looks of youth, but the knowledge of the ages.

Naturally, we also have an illustration of the love of music incorporated in this card, together with the simple joy of life.

Inexperience and childlike innocence reveal a mind which is not closed to unusual experiences, since it has not yet learned of the perils of the world.

Here can be the thoughts of a person chasing the elusive butterfly, whether of love or intuition (love if the Union card is close by, and intuition if the Stars is adjacent), though being unaware of the chaos and anarchy often left in his wake. Also represented here is the eternal day dreamer wishing to stay out of the rat race with no malice of heart - plus the symbolism of Buddhism and meditation.

The Fool is often unaffected by rules and regulations, which is displayed by a line up of Scales, Sage, Work, Tower and the Fool, but he often narrowly misses pitfalls in this way, and this is indicated when the previous cards are followed by Destruction and Liberation.

You will find that a ragamuffin is also defined in this card, those who do not care what they look like, but have a heart of gold - they just do not want to be tied down by materialism. This is implied by his unkempt clothes and the movement away from the house.

Now, gazing at the building in the background, you may be led to thoughts of ancient places and the deep love of architecture from times gone by. Then, if the Destruction and Beast cards are present, at the same moment your intuition may imply the foundations of something about to give way or show that you have now to move away from the brink, thus learning to step over obstacles.

When the Querent is looking into problems concerning relationships, and the fool follows the cards signifying the persons concerned, it would indicate that one of them definitely prefers to be out and about rather than at home, thus showing the possible cause of the trouble.

the beast

33. THE BEAST

The Querent often dislikes the hostile look of this card at first glance, as it displays that spiteful, beastly side of our nature which we would prefer to hide. The sinister shades of red come into their full sybolic use within the Beast card, from cruelty, greed and anger to lust and desire. Well suited to this pictorial display of Man's worst aspects are the darker blended oranges of pride and the surroundings in muddy tints, symbolising low intellect. Have care that the claws and teeth do not get a grip on you; tread carefully. You may need to make a voyage of discovery in order to learn what the Beast is within yourself. More often than not, we also try to cover it up with rose-tinted lenses.

Initially, of course, the Beast represents the worst side of a being's nature, the side we need to learn about and control, yet if it stands for someone else in our life within a spread, there is an obvious warning here.

Look underneath the Beast and see the blue, the red having given thoughts of temper with an excess of energy. The blue is a toning influence, the softer side of a hard person's nature, perhaps. However remember also that when this card appears it is a warning first, often of a confrontation with an unpleasant person (possibly with a bad temper and spiteful nature), therefore it is necessary to notice the blue, suggesting the need to look for a weak spot.

In a spread with the Body, Tower, Wheel and Libido, the beast card indicates that the hard outer shell of the dragon needs to be removed in order to assist the Beast to become the beautiful creature. One also has to question the reasoning behind doing so, and how much violence you can take in aggravating the Beast enough to make him see what he is really like. The Beast is, of course, a card with a negative vibration which spells danger and excess, so, if in a spread following the Voyage, Libido and the Message, it indicates that the expected voyage of discovery and anticipated joy will have an unexpectedly disastrous finish, probably due to an excessive temper. However, in a different order, such as Beast, Voyage, Libido and Message, it would indicate a forceful obstacle in your path which is going to prove difficult to pass - is it worth it? If so, you must endeavour to overcome it.

Now, if the Fortune card is followed by the Beast and the Message, the interpretation would be of a material greed needing to be altered.

The symbology of the Beast in a layout with the Peace and Stars could quite easily be one of the powerful dark forces unleashing their destructive influence in your peaceful life and beyond.

Occasionally, in a spread showing the Beast, Libido, Cave and Union, it has been known to imply a spiteful side to the physical sexual side of a relationship.

HAPPENINGS

Throughout our lives, instances and situations will occur which will transform us, often intervening when least expected. These 'happenings' are symbolised in the following cards.

We may be occupied elsewhere when MESSAGES, VOYAGES, and PUZZLES unexpectedly demand our attention. We may feel we are in a PRISON when suddenly LIBERATION appears. The depressions of the CAVE may engulf us only shortly before the joys represented by the UNION card are ours.

Each card adds vital information to the rest of the deck, thus each being dependent upon the others.

34. THE MESSAGE

A lifeline and a promise are included in this card. Here, the planks of a ship are shown in a glorious yellowy-orange which interprets within colour consciousness, as a symbol of generosity. The net is full, containing fish in a beautiful, healing blue. This theme is expanded upon in the green seaweed, together with the colour of the bottle in rejuvenating shades.

A very intriguing card with many a message, such as "the catch being drawn in"; "the message hidden in a bottle"; "rope being thrown to catch", or "look amongst the woodwork." Life is full of surprises, and this is indicated by the appearance of this particular card in the spread.

If this card appears, there is a promise of important tidings, and it usually signifies plenty to come if it appears in the future position.

Within the pictorial illustration of the Message, you will be drawn to the thoughts of fishermen and the sea. Also, through the symbology of the design itself, there are connections with Christianity; this would be emphasised by the presence of the Peace card. However, if this card is preceded by the Voyage, then your interpretation could be of the hobby of sailing, or of yachts. Alternatively, should the cards be reversed, the signal would be of news concerning a voyage, or a letter from abroad.

In a layout which shows the Message and Fortune together, they will increase the leanings towards thoughts of a gain in the way of treasures.

The Message card is often an indication of success,such as certificates or positive examination results on their way; thus, when the Sage is present, it indicates good marks at the end of studies. Although if the Home card is also in the same layout, the Message may well be of deeds or legal papers concerning the property to be dealt with. Yet there are times when a spread gives us the Home, Union, Death, Birth, Sage and Message cards, that the solution is appertaining to a divorce.

When the Message is followed by the Puzzle in this particular line up, it is indicative of a hold up in the papers and, if the Puzzle is replaced by the Beast, it would stand for a delay in the proceedings. Therefore, other cards are definitely necessary to give the Message card its fullest interpretation.

Sometimes the Message card implies that the Querent needs to contact others or is perhaps hiding something away, and both of these meanings would be the theme if the Cave is adjacent to the Message card.

Another direction in which this card can take you is to the intuitive level, when indications to look within are suggested, especially if the Cave and Libido are laid in the same position.

35. THE VOYAGE

Sparkling blue sea and sky make your journey in this galleon a pleasure and sure to be one of exciting adventures. The two-dimensional quality of this card allows you to look at your voyage from a stand point of more than one level, from the romantic swashbuckling degree to the articulate practical planning areas. Hence the movement can be through the everyday trials to the spiritually philosophical aspects - life can be a puzzle! The light blue in this card is a true illustration, within the colour awareness concepts, of hope.

Life is the voyage that first comes to my mind when glancing at this card, and one can start to understand its further direction when one considers its position - past, present or future?

Initially, a card of movement - travel - in some direction, but obviously bringing to the conscious mind thought of foreign lands, new places, peoples and experiences. Of course, the actual voyage may just be within oneself, across the uncharted seas of the inner world of the pysche into the metaphysical dimensions.

Naturally, on the surface, the Voyage card symbolises a love of the sea and, therefore, links with the navy; yet, on a smaller scale, it can also represent model ship builders. Now, the ship itself is seen through an ancient map, which can indicate a collector of antique maps (which we see advertised everywhere nowadays), or as the professions, such as cartography and map curators. Perhaps in the future, when sitting next to the Moon card in a spread, this card will mean a Voyage to the Moon! However, these same cards together for the moment represent a journey through our own emotional self.

When the Voyage card is in a layout together with the Liberation card, the implications are that an acquaintance is moving away. A journey which you would prefer not to take is indicated when the Voyage card is between the Beast and Destruction cards. Should the Voyage follow the Fool and Liberation cards, it would imply that the Querent was of a restless nature and seeking an adventure in a new avenue but if they were also followed by the Stars, the suggestion would be that the Querent was really going places! We all know those people with grand visions of far places who never actually

succeed; well, this could be defined in a spread including a line up of Peace, Stars, Voyage Never and Fool cards.

Finally let your eyes drift to the fancy star shaped cartouche in the right-hand corner, and then slip into a meditative state allowing the card to trigger those illusive thoughts of distant imaginings of strange dimensions and planets.

36. THE PUZZLE

The only card in the Psycard deck which is turned on its side but, of course, it is the Puzzle and fully the puzzle in its pictorial entirety. When in a muddle, on whatever level, we need to be practical in our approach, and this is brought into play in the colour concepts of the card by the clear brown of the trees and doors; but if unable to sort the puzzle out, we feel trapped and imprisoned.

Notice the statue-like quality of the Queen holding out the key to a locked door, then ponder on the game of chess and the role of the Queen as the power behind the ruler - as the person who holds the key to the mysteries behind the door - but which one, which square leads the way?

A design of trees laid on the chequered floor gives alternating balance with reflected knowledge, due to this design being a reflection of the trees above. The trees themselves at first appear real, and then the trunks show precision in their form to add to the thoughts that a puzzle needs careful consideration. However, notice that there are differences in every tree and that the paths are not the mirror images of one's first impressions, also the floor designs differ, hence the necessity to consider the alternatives very carefully.

A very difficult card when in play, since it is often a card which blocks the opening up of the question which is being asked, as it still leaves the choice to the fore. Which door does the key open, which one should you choose? The choice is yours.

Time and time again we are faced with situations where we are forced to make an agonising decision and usually there is no clue given as to which course is most suitable to take. The Puzzle card is symbolic of these situations, the time to choose, to try and get out of the tangle. It is the card of challenges and riddles which have always faced man, especially through the mythic figures of our ancient tales, but they are also there in our everyday lives.

Sometimes this card shows a need to step carefully through the pattern of life, and can be the obstacle that threatens to defeat you, especially when surrounded by the Destruction and Beast cards.

However, a small plaque hanging on the tree - which at times looks like a puzzle with an eye and yet another time a fish - perhaps brings forward thoughts of the "all seeing eye" and the "fish" of religion, signifying further influences to be considered.

The circles within this plaque all overlap at one point, thus showing all areas of life seemingly encroaching on each other. The Puzzle represents confusion in all areas whenever it appears in a spread, and is instrumental in opening out or blocking the full interpretation of other cards. However, they in themselves do little or nothing to alter this card's own meaning.

A very interesting card to use in meditation - try opening the doors!

37. PRISON

A splash of ethereal blue shines through the open grill to brighten our cell with a promise of hope, yet we sit there in total dejection not noticing its rays. Stout bars cover the entrance but it appears that if we would only look around we should see that they are well spaced and there is again hope of freedom, but we must realise this before we can truly seek our liberation.

Normally one has to explain to a sitter that - no, this does not indicate an actual prison. However, I have had this card appear within the spread of a prison visitor, a police officer and when a prison sentence was awaited! So beware not to let yourself fall into the trap of getting too used to the same repetitive patter! Naturally, it is more likely to be the feeling of someone in a depressing position or possibly a confining situation.

At times the empty bowl is really large and one has to explain to the Querent that the shackles are self-imposed.

It is one of those cards which becomes easier to interpret when appearing in a spread with additional cards, since they will help to define in which areas the Querent is trapped or trapping others.

The squared floor of the cell symbolises foundations. However, this time they appear to be of the type which restrict you, due to the density of their format. Since the blocks of the wall do not appear to be in true formation, the walls imply that although the foundations were correct you have deviated from the plan; hence all the indications point to a blindness to the true situation.

When the Prison card follows Union, but precedes Liberation, the layout implies that the Querent has a relationship which is confusing which they wish to be freed from. However, if the card representing the Inquirer is followed by the Union, Libido and Prison cards, the implications here are that the Querent's personality traits are restricting a partner in a relationship.

We can all feel trapped by a working situation and this would be illustrated, of course, by the presence of the Work card together with the Prison. Now, should the Prison card appear in a layout with the Sage, Skills, Cave and

Destruction, there are significant indications that there could be possible confinement due to a court case.

Should a display appear including the Peace, Warrior and Prison cards, it could signify that the person in question had a rather strict and confined idealism concerning religion.

38. LIBERATION

All life has its prisons and journeys through experience. At some time all the colourful aspects of life will affect us, whereby we seek liberation in some manner or another. Here, within this card, we have finally sought a liberation, yet the door lock appears to be a false one. So what was really holding us? The emerald green of the grass comes forward to revitalise us for our journey out of the material shades of the castle, over the bridge and into the shades of delicate change and....?

Often, one is trying to find the way out of a particular situation in which one is seemingly trapped, and there is a need to turn to another for assistance - perhaps even a new sphere of life. The key is in the lock, yet no sign of a bolt gives the realisation that the liberation sought is really within ones power to achieve, and often just a matter of looking for it.

Initially, then, this is the card symbolising the joyous release from captivity - the freedom to start afresh or change paths. It defines the transition period away from constricting influences. However, occasionally, there is an indication of a warning with the card of a need to have care in the sense of being led astray - off of one's planned path, for example, in a layout of the Work, Liberation, Stranger and Beast cards. There are times in our lives when we need to be advised to release ourselves from guilt feelings, and this would be implied in a line up of the Beast, Libido, Prison and Liberation following after the card representing the Querent.

See the two travellers on horseback fleeing over the bridge - this particular aspect has been known to signify people who have eloped especially when in a spread with the Peace and Union cards. The Liberation card represents freedom of thought and action, a time to give thanks that bad times are past. However, in a spread concerning a family unit it, often signifies that someone is shortly to leave the family nest. I have also found that a group showing the Peace, Stars, Sage, Birth and Liberation cards will illustrate the birth of a new freedom of thought on philosophical lines.

The Liberation card is excellent in a layout questioning a health condition, since it symbolises a release from the restrictions of the illness.

39. THE CAVE

So many times in our lives we have sought freedom from our prison only to be thrown into a more depressing situation. This is well depicted within the design and colourings of this card. All the dark shades of despair and depression are there, yet is there a hint of better times on their way from outside of the cave if only we look around the corner? Perhaps we need to create a Union between our higher self and the physical, thereby forming the balance of our being.

A picture of many shadowy areas forming various shapes for the mind to play on. See the shadows forming a reclining body on the wall of the cave, sometimes these shadows appear like the female womb and give thoughts of pregnancy, the curled up form giving one thoughts of depression and a desperate hiding away from the world of light - thus occasionally showing a fear of facing up to problems.

This card represents the depressed state, the suffering of self due to unhappy times. It can also signify introversion and loneliness, but also acts as a reminder to the Inquirer that the light is there waiting, following a period of rest in the darkness. Withdrawal is also symbolised in this card but it must be also remembered that this is sometimes a healing process.

Occasionally, when the question pertains to a health condition, and the Cave card appears along with the Body and Destruction cards, the indications are of a mental breakdown. Yet if the person in question is a female and just the Body card is laid together with the Cave, it will imply an internal problem healthwise and possibly point to the reproductive organs. Naturally, other themes for this card are those of shyness, a fear of facing others or oneself and, if in a spread with the Libido and Skills, it would signify a time to come out into the daylight, throw off the shyness and have confidence.

Also included in the symbology of the Cave card is the uncertainty and sometimes apprehension we have of the unknown, whether it be the world, ourselves or other dimensions. Yet often it implies a fear of the world with an acceptance of the realms of astral light. Sometimes, when doing a reading for a male and the Libido sits beside the Cave and Beauty cards, it brings forth a shyness of the female species.

40. UNION

Blue and white waters flow down the fasciated stream, perhaps bringing that Union of the Self into being. As always, throughout time there are little rocks over which the stream of our life has to travel. Varying shades of green softly cover the ground through which our stream flows, and here we find the grail chalice of the Fortune card out in the open, just waiting for us to pick it up. The cup always links to affairs of the heart.

Look at the depth of the crevices through which the river flows sometimes deep and then shallow, just as in life. Of course, your eyes play tricks and at times the river flows together, yet on other occasions it moves apart - whichever way you sense it in a specific reading, it is indicative of the way a relationship is going.

There can be a flow of ideas into the melting pot of the bubbling waters at the centre of the card, obviously giving the interpretation that the ideas need to be mixed and assimilated.

This card firstly stands for a coming together, the alliance or marriage, of people or ideas. It is a symbolic representation of a celebration and relationship. Within all this, it can signify the merging of our various personality traits into a totally co-ordinated being.

One must be careful when talking of relationships not to imply that it is necessarily a love-link; use your intuition properly. The Union can be between business partners, boss and employee, child and parent, or even just friendships of a close nature.

A card which represents a meaning to life for many - happiness and affection, or even marriage.

The Friendship card following the Union may just symbolise togetherness in a very pleasant sharing way. Yet the Union following Friendship implies that from a friendship has grown a loving, caring relationship which has the potential of marriage (we should also remember that marriage is simply the sharing of a life style by two people and not always the signed piece of paper).

When the Union card is laid in a spread following the Peace, Beast, Fool and Liberation, it would indicate a reconciliation between two people.

Now, should the Body and Destruction cards precede the Union card we would be wise to interpret this as the health and mental states of the person in question as now being well on the way to recovery and balance, through Union of its inner aspects.

When the Peace card precedes Union, it would illustrate a reconciliation of a person's spiritual concepts. Still on these themes, the Union is also symbolic of a person's spiritual quest or path. One final snippet - I was told by another consultant in a reading for himself that in a line up of the Union, Sun and Work cards it was defined, after much deliberation and time, to symbolise that he would not get a job with the "Sun" newspaper until his Union card was up to date!

COLOUR INTERPRETATIONS

Thankfully, we are becoming more aware of the importance of colour consciousness in our lives, and alert to the effects of colouring our surroundings.

The interpretation of colour varies depending upon its environment and also in the seer's eyes. Colour will refer to one thing within an aura when relating it to health conditions, but something entirely different if elucidating upon the personality's character qualities. However, the effect of colour in our clothes and decor, once again, brings forward the balancing healing effects; of course, here the colours may also be interpreted in another way! Therefore, it is important to develop your own personal symbolic meanings.

I must state here that, when seeing the colour illuminations of 'Spiritual Guides' it should not be assumed that the colour definitions are the same as any listed here; the interpretations must come from their dimensions.

I list here my own definitions of colours which can be seen in the Psycards, in the hope that it will assist you to evolve personal explanations in all areas. To add to your awareness of the effects that colours have on you when worn, I also list a few of the benefits.

Black	Malice, Vice, Deprivation, Heavy Materiality
Reddish Black	Vicious, Evil
Clear Bright Blue	Loyalty
Cobalt Blue	Purpose
Dark Blue	Spiritual Questing
Deep Sky Blue	Inspiration
Delicate Blue	Healing
Dusky Blue	Devotion smothered
Light Blue	Hope
Radiant Blue	Healing
Rich Blue	Forcefulness
Soft Ethereal Blue	Devotion
Turquoise	Seeking maturity
Clear Brown	Avarice
Donkey Brown	Earthy practicality
Dull Grey-Brown	Selfishness
Light Brown	General practicality
Warm and Soft Brown	Protection
Gold Pure	Sincerity
Apple Green	Sympathetic humanitarian ideals
Bottle Green	Negativity
Dark Blue-Green	Soul Searching
Deep Green	Lack of confidence
Delicate Green	Peacefulness
Dull Clear Green	Calmness
Emerald Green	Regeneration, Rejuvenation
Grassy Green	Harmony
Light Green	Success
Lime Green	Positivity
Mid Green	Versatility
Olive Green	Treachery
Soft Blue-Green	Mentally calming

130

Vivid Green	Creativity
Yellowy-Green	Daydreamer
Brownish-Grey	Depression
Dark Grey	Lack of imagination
Light Grey	Fear
Opaque Grey	Dullness
Mauves	Spiritual Motives
Pinky-Mauve	Cosmic Consciousness with Emotions
Bright Orange	Etheric Energy
Burnt Orange	Vitality
Clear Orange	Materially motivated Alertness
Deep Orange	Pride
Muddy Orange	Low Intellect
Yellowy-Orange	Generosity
Pink	Unselfish Love
Delicate Pink	Modesty
Brick Red	Aggression
Bright Red	Vitality, Positiveness
Clear Red	Ambition and Energy
Cloudy Red	Greed
Crimson Red	Sensuality
Deep Red	Love OR Anger
Deep rich Red	Lust
Pinky-Red	Vital life Force
Rosy Red	Warm Characteristics
Silver	Vivacity but can be fickleness
White	Purity, Cosmic Awareness
Bright Yellow	Intellectual Power
Clear Golden Yellow	High Soul Qualities
Dark Yellow	Jealousy
Dingy Yellow	Suspicion
Dull Yellow	False Optimism

Greeny-Yellow	Nervousness
Sandy Shades	Strong ideals on a Practical level
Sharp Yellow	Teaching Qualities
Lemon Yellow	Mental Alertness

WEARING COLOURS

Blues	General Healing, self-reliant Peacefulness
Browns	Security, materiality, organisation
Greens	Harmony, calmness, balance, growth
Oranges	Vitality, cheerfulness, fearlessness
Pinks	Loving, gentleness, affectionate
Purples	Sensitivity, dignity, originality
Reds	Energy, courage, vigorous, strength
Yellows	Well-being, intellectual, joyful, imaginative

DIVINATORY METHODS

INTRODUCTION TO DIVINATORY METHODS

This section is dedicated to the Psycards being used in conjunction with one another, in the form of patterns which are commonly called 'spreads' or 'layouts'. It is essential, if you are attempting to expand your usage and understanding of the language of the Psycards, to develop a fluid and lucid knowledge of their complete interplay amongst themselves and the cycle of life in its fullest concept.

From the dawn of time, man has tried to understand himself and the universe around him. Also, within this struggle, there has always grown a desire to see the patterns of the past together with the mistakes, yet again to question the future paths available. Propagating from this came a variety of divinatory forms which ranged from the usage of seeds to bones and yarrow sticks. However, there also came the Seers with their far-sightedness and voices. It was found that, generally, common man preferred to see Mystics use an instrument and symbols, hence the ancients' Emerald Crystal Balls, Sand and Pyromancy.

In spite of all this, there still needs to be a method of interpretation to cover all the requirements of man's questioning mind, hence there was always a necessity for a basic plan to facilitate each 'Query'. Whatever is used needs to have an initial meaning for where the instruments land, to expand upon the instruments' own definition. In this way, there came about the birth of divinatory methods/spreads/layouts/operations!

Amongst the following methods there will be found ways of interpreting the cards in the simplest of ideas for those of you who are just starting out upon your investigatory path. Then again, there are spreads included for the experienced 'Reader' in order to make the reading of this book an enlightening experience for all. I must reiterate especially here within the following pages, that all of you are classed as 'Readers' and that the 'Querent' or 'Inquirer' becomes your problem and situation, therefore, if you are reading your own cards, you become as two persons yourself. Obviously, if you are actually doing a 'reading' for someone else they in reality become the 'Querent'.

134

THE STAR

The following method is a useful sequence which will assist you to define a variety of aspects influencing your life but can be adapted to fit a situation. Place the Inquirer card in the centre of the table, face upwards, and shuffle the cards. Now deal the cards face upwards in the pattern and order shown below:

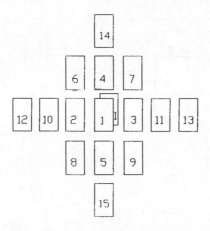

To interpret the cards, it is an advantage to proceed in the same order in which they were laid and commence to expand upon their meanings by using the following key:-

The cards which are placed closest to the Inquirer are the influences nearest your heart or have the first effects on the situation. The cards which sit in the positions 10-13 are those coming in to affect your life very shortly. Now the card in position no. 14 is representative of your outer projection or goal, whilst that at position no. 15 stands for the underlying factor and/or influences.

By way of expanding the reading, you may wish to include, within the basic position-meanings, the concept that generally the cards in the vertical column (which includes the Inquirer Card) are the present. The cards to the left of this column then become the past whilst those to the right stand for the future.

THE VITAL SEVEN

This is the easiest spread in the book to read, since there are so few cards to interpret.

Place the Inquirer card in the centre of the table and shuffle the deck. Lay two cards above the Inquirer face down, then one card to the left and one to the right of the Inquirer, followed by two cards placed below, as displayed here:

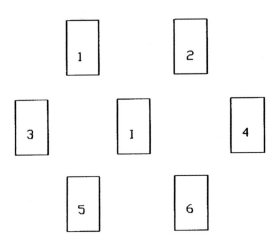

Continue by interpreting the spread by using the simple key that the top two cards equal the past, the middle line represents the present, whereas the bottom cards show the future. Also that which is on the left is influencing you, and what is on the right is that which you are influencing.

It is suggested that you turn each card over and interpret individually, then look at the overall picture.

THE DECISION MAKER

When you have a difficult decision to make, the cards can help you quite simply and in an easy manner.

Place the Inquirer on the table and shuffle the cards whilst concentrating upon your question clear and precise in your mind without changing it's format.

Lay the first seven cards from the top of the deck in a horizontal line and read your answer:

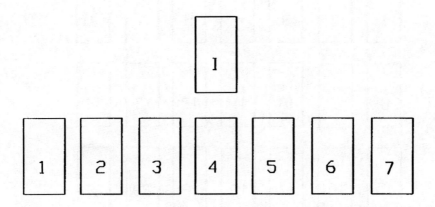

Within the seven cards, there should be a key-card which is extremely relevant to your question, then another giving the answer.

Should there be no relevant answer, it simply means that this is not the correct time to ask - try again another day!

TRADITIONAL 21 CARD DISPLAY

You will no doubt have seen the following layout used in a variety of divinatory books. It is a very good spread for general reading, but it is usually advisable to take cards numbered 1-5 out and lay them aside, until you have familiarised yourself with the Psycards. Shuffle the pack well and lay a row of seven cards on the table from left to right, follow this by laying a second and third row of seven cards, each in the same manner:

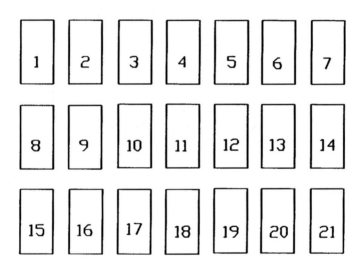

Interpret the cards by stating that the first row represents the past, the second row stands for the present, whilst the last and bottom row shows the future. To extend the spread, it is then possible to read the cards in threes in a downward process to see the individual influences of the past over the present and future, i.e. cards 1,8,& 15; then cards 2,9,&16; and so on.

A variation on this spread's interpretation is to look for a theme card in each individual line and let the intuitive/psychic self give the conscious you the correct solution.

WEEKLY SEVEN

We are all tempted by something or another to see into the week ahead, the immediate future but in a generalised way, hence the following spread was born to assist in that process.

The spread is quite simple and generally it should be read in a light-hearted manner straight off the top of the cards, as one would say! Shuffle the pack and lay seven cards in the order shown - one card in each position:

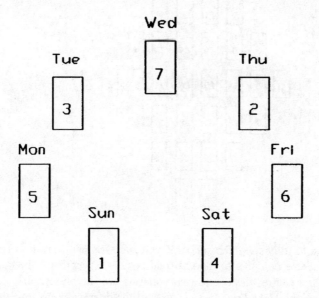

Read the cards in the order shown. The first to be interpreted obviously needs to be that one in position representing the day of the week relevant to the day upon which you are doing your reading; or the following day. Remember, that the interpretation for the Day is just to give you an idea of what might possibly appear. However, should you wish to go into more depth for your week, lay a pile of three cards in each position, and use a group for the particular day.

THE DIAMOND

Here is a layout which is especially beneficial in assisting your own intuition to grow and thereby use the Psycards as triggers to your own psyche. Remove the Inquirer card as it is not used in this spread, now shuffle the deck and lay the cards in the pattern shown:

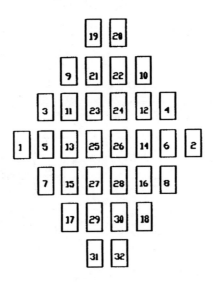

It will assist you to fully solve the spread if you learn the basic position key as follows. The three columns to the left (odd nos. 1-17) represent the past going towards the centre; the centre two columns are the present and the three columns to the right (even nos. 2-18) stand for movement into the future.

When commencing the interpretation of the actual pictures, remember the position, e.g. perhaps in the past, and then let the picture talk to you as though associated with the past, e.g. The Stars card followed by Death, could mean an outstanding opportunity which was lost or collapsed in the past.

There will be seven cards left which may be used to answer a question which arises from the spread.

THE CROSS

Now for a spread which is especially good when you wish to let the cards themselves talk to you. It will assist you to learn their language by giving you key cards every time you lay the pattern out, and provide the theme for that particular five-card display. It is possible to work with just one layout of five cards, or to extend the reading by continuing the pattern until the whole deck has been interpreted. However, you will find that there are four cards left over which become a final summary for the future. This spread is a particular favourite of mine and 1 would expect you to have some very surprisingly lucid results.

Place the Inquirer Card in the centre of the table then shuffle the deck thoroughly whilst clearing your mind and settling down, or if you are doing a 'reading' for someone else, concentrate on the Querent generally. However, it will assist you immensely when reading for a 'Querent' or using the whole pack, to state in your mind that those cards laid at the beginning of the spread represent the deepest past and the rest of the pack will work through to the last cards, representing the future. Deal the first five cards in the arrangement as indicated and commence to elucidate on them in the order which they are laid, but loosely:

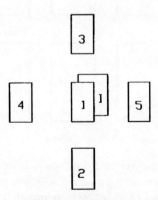

The card which is placed on top of the Inquirer card represents you/the Querent or the centre of the Situation. That which is in position no.2 portrays what is the underlying factor; position no.3 equals the goal; whereas no.4 shows the past influences and that in place no.5 is the future outcome.

THE TWELVE MONTHS

This is a spread which is quite simple to learn and enables you to see a pattern formulating over a long period of time, whereby assisting you to prepare yourself for possible events.

Shuffle the deck and lay a row made up of 4 piles of three cards, then lay a second and third row in the same manner, so that each place shown below represents a pile of three cards on your table (each letter represents three cards):

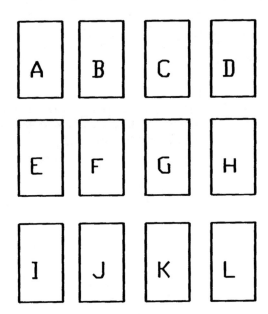

When interpreting the spread, you would normally commence with the first set laid as representing the month following that which you are in. However, if you are within the first half of the current month, it is permissible to read the first set of three cards as symbolic of that month and continuing from that month onwards. The last four cards can be used to answer a specific question that might have arisen out of the displayed cards.

STAR OF DAVID SPREAD

This is another spread which enables Psycards to actually speak to you. By just asking within one's mind 'What is around this person?' whilst you are shuffling the cards and then laying them, you will find that the patterns together with the cards dictate the interpretation of each individual six cards.

Place the Inquirer card in the centre but only to mark the position. Shuffle the cards and place them in positions and order as displayed here:

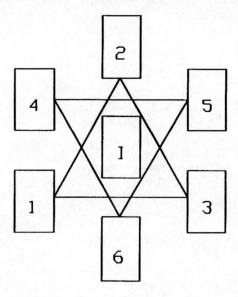

To solve the meaning of this spread, allow your intuitive mind free rein on each individual card and then over the total patterns. However, to extend the reading continue to lay six cards at a time in the same manner, and interpret each set individually right through the whole pack. It is quite likely that you will find a link forming easily between each set of six cards if you allow your imagination and intuition to formulate your words even as you commence to lay the new set.

143

THIRTY-FIVE CARD BLOCK

Of course, there are those readers and sitters who like to see a lot of cards on the table in order to show a flow and clearly developing display. Therefore, this easily laid spread is ideal and it can be interpreted, to a lesser or greater extent as desired. However, I would add that this particular display can easily take an hour or more to interpret fully.

Firstly, remove the Inquirer and Direction cards (i.e. nos. 1-5) then shuffle the remaining cards. Lay them face downwards in five columns of seven cards vertically as shown below:

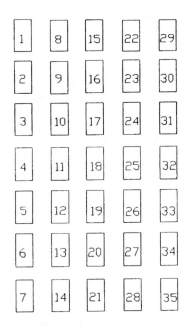

Read the cards in the same order in which they were laid, using the following key to assist your interpretation.

Cards 1-7   The past causes of your character.
Cards 8-14   The General past.
Cards 15-21   The present time.
Cards 22-28   The future trends.
Cards 29-35   The future themes and obstacles to be aware of.

Once you have deciphered the spread, you may desire to extend it by reading the cards across the lines (horizontally), i.e. 1-29, followed by 2-30 and so on. However, when interpreting the cards this time, it is imperative to look for a key card in each individual line to give the basis for that specific row's topic.

PYRAMID

Now this is a particularly useful layout (see previous page) that can be easily adapted to understand the background and progression of a particular aspect, such as doing the spread to find out the spiritual or relationship direction. Therefore, you may change the specific meanings of the individual card positions, although still keeping the basic meanings of each row the same.

You may find it advantageous to remove the Inquirer and Direction cards and put them aside, prior to commencing this display, but the choice is entirely up to you, although it is suggested that you practice both ways first.

Shuffle the cards and then lay in the pattern as shown on the previous page, reading them in the same order as they are laid. The following suggestions for basic individual position definitions may help you to interpret the spread initially:

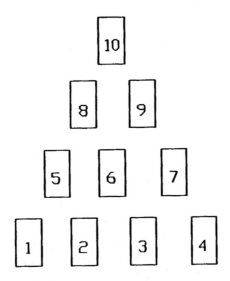

Key:

Bottom Row - Background Aspects:-

1	Family
2	Personality/Schooling
3	Spiritual/Religious Foundations
4	Work

Second Row - Current Trends:-

5	Family
6	Inner Self
7	Work

Third Row - Future Possibilities:-

8	Family
9	Work

Top Card

10	Outcome of Self

ARROW HEAD

An unusual layout which I have personally used in order to answer specific questions that still need to have their causes and origins explained.

Place the Inquirer card in the centre of the table and remove from the deck the Direction cards nos. 2-5, as they are not used in this method. Shuffle the deck and place the cards in the manner shown:

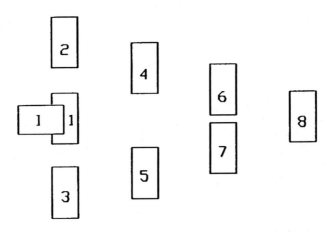

Use the key opposite to help you solve the meanings that are in the cards, but remember to allow your own intuition to flow.

Key:

i. The card which falls into position 8 is your actual answer.

ii. Positions 2 & 3 are the distant past.

iii. Places 4 & 5 are the past and current affects and effects.

iv. Whereas those cards in positions 6 & 7 show the current and future trends.

v. The card which represents the character of the querent; the core of the question or situation is card no.1 which covers the Inquirer card.

A. The overriding / crowning factors are the cards sitting in positions 2,4 & 6.

B. Whilst the cards place in positions 3, 5 & 7 show the underlying causes and reasons.

All the cards laid should show you clearly all the facets behind the answer to your question and why it is advisable to accept it's decision.

THE FAN

This spread may assist a person to find possible solutions to the situation they are presently in by constructing a picture which illustrates the pattern of progression in various aspects of their life.

Firstly, take out the Inquirer card and place at the bottom of the table, then shuffle the pack whilst concentrating upon the querent or the situation in question, proceeding by laying the cards in the arrangement below forming the fan shape:

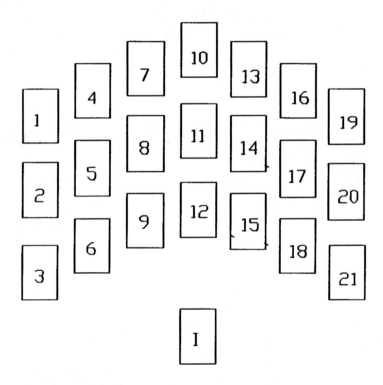

Now commence to interpret the spread by using the key opposite for the respective positions. However, read this fully before actually starting the interpretation.

Key:

1   Parents and childhood, preterite family conditions.
2   Parents and teens - past family situations.
3   - present family conditions.

4	Character / emotional self	- background.
5		- present state.
6		- possible future developments.

7	Current family/relationship	- background.
8		- present situation.
9		- future changes.

10	Religious / spiritual	- upbringing.
11		- inner aspirations/changes.
12		- possible achievement to aim for.

13	Work	- background.
14		- present aspirations.
15		- possible future achievements.

16 Current trends.
17 Immediate future trends.
18 Long term trends.

19}
20} Possible unseen obstacles or success to come.
21}

THE PENTAGRAM

The following design has been incorporated within the process of a variety of divinatory systems and tools by psychics, and seems to be a favourite due to its magical connotations. However, it proves to be an interesting design to work with in a purely mundane way and we give here two variations for the solution of your spread. Firstly, place the Inquirer card on the table to mark the central point. Shuffle the pack and deal the cards into the positions as if you were actually drawing a Pentagram then a final card over the Inquirer:

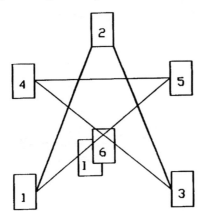

To read the spread, interpret the cards laying in positions 4 & 1 as representing the past, the cards in positions 5 & 3 as the future, then the card at the top in position no. 2 shows your aims. However, the extra card laid over the Inquirer always stands for your personal traits, whether you are aware of them or not. The second variation to expand, or give a different slant to your solving the layout is to follow the first interpretation with another incorporating the Elements normally associated with the Pentagram. I have listed here the Elements together with a few key words to assist:

Card	Element	Associated Words
2	Spirit	Light, Source, Essence, Spiritual Love.
4	Water	Emotion, Fluid/Stagnant, Feelings.
5	Air	Mental, Conversation, Thought, Vibration.
1	Earth	Material, Work, Pressure, Food, Physical.
3	Fire	Energy, Force, Violence, Drive, Movement.

PILLARS OF LIFE

The spread described here was created by Ian Watt, and I am positive that once you have learnt the process, you will find it gives great pleasure within its development. The key is actually used throughout the Pillars of Life spread and it is quite simple to remember; however, the first complete pattern of thirteen cards (when all laid) relates to the past, whereas the second pattern of twenty-one cards which completes the spread, flows forward into the future.

Take the Inquirer Card and place it on the table in the centre top. Shuffle the deck and commence to lay the cards for the first pattern, from left to right by laying the first three cards one after another in a horizontal line to the left of the Inquirer. Then lay a fourth card over the Inquirer on its own in the centre. Now lay a further three cards in a horizontal line to the right of the Inquirer. Interpret this row first. The cards on the left represent the physical side of your life, while the middle line (covering the Inquirer) symbolises your True Self. The cards laid to form the right pillar stand for the spiritual side of your nature.

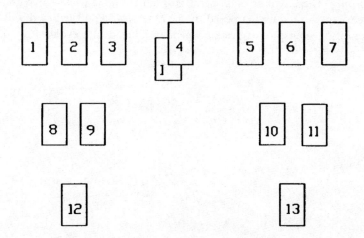

Follow this line by placing two cards to the left underneath the original three; two cards to the right underneath those for the spiritual side and interpret these on their own. To finish laying the first pattern - on a third line place a further card on each side below those already on the table and once again, give the meanings separately. You will now have formed the first pattern as drawn above. However, it will be found that, when you have deciphered the cards in the manner stated in individual lines, it is possible to see a new interplay between all of those now laid and relevant information can be discerned.

Now that you have deciphered this part of the layout, we continue to complete the spread with the second pattern in the following way.

Take the cards which you have already laid on the left of the Inquirer and draw them up into a pile still on the left but with the last card laid (no. 12) placed on the top. Follow the same procedure for the cards laid to the right on the Inquirer so that the top card is no 13. This will give you three separate positions with the top cards laid in positions (12), (4), and (13) showing. Proceed to lay cards under those already on the table to form three pillars so that each card is visible, by placing a card at a time on each pillar in turn until there is a total of seven cards in each line (overleaf).

Just let your mind flow as you move down the columns to interpret their meanings fully. There will be eight cards still left from the pack - seven of which are to answer a question posed by the Querent, and a final card will give the reply to the unspoken question which we all tend not to voice.

Physical Side   True Self   Spiritual Side

| 12 | | 4 | | 13 |

| 14 | | 15 | | 16 |

| 17 | | 18 | | 19 |

| 20 | | 21 | | 22 |

| 23 | | 24 | | 25 |

| 26 | | 27 | | 28 |

| 29 | | 30 | | 31 |

PASCAL'S TRIANGLE

This spread is loosely based on Pascal's Triangle, which was first used by Omar Khayyam, and although it may appear complicated at first, it is excellent for showing direction together with guidance. It is a method which starts from the present stand-point and, therefore, is only designed to show you the future.

Place the Inquirer card at the centre top of the table and shuffle the rest of the pack whilst concentrating upon the question under consideration. Now commence to lay the cards by laying the first one over the Inquirer card and completing the layout in the exact order shown in the diagram, i.e. increasing each row by two cards.

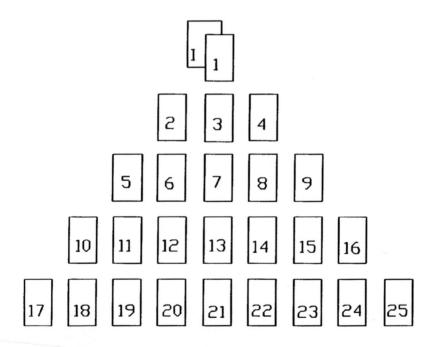

When you begin to interpret the spread, the cards must be read in a downward manner and it is important to digest the key first (see opposite).

Key:

Card No.1 represents you and the present state. Follow this by interpreting the positions 1, 3, 7, 13 & 21 as a flow through showing the immediate pathway ahead which you are currently upon. Continue by deciphering the cards in positions 1, 2, 5, 10 & 17 which show your karmic pathway which is available. Now read the cards numbered 1, 4, 9, 16 & 25 to show the alternative / New material path open to you, the Inquirer.

Always when taking a new path in life there is a desire to know not only what is ahead but what one should do to oneself to achieve the change.

So now interpret the cards 6, 11, 18, 12, 19 & 20 in this order, to show you the requirements needed to achieve your karmic path and whether advisable. Likewise read 8, 15, 24, 14, 23 & 22 in said order to give you the necessary changes required to achieve the new material path if suitable.

THE GRAND STAR

The following divinatory operation is ideal for a comprehensive reading with enough cards remaining to answer questions which may arise in the Inquirer's mind following the interpretation, whilst leaving the spread upon the table for further discussion. However, this is not considered a spread to work with until you have learnt the language of the Psycards.

To start, place the Inquirer Card in the middle of the table and shuffle the pack thoroughly while concentrating upon the Querent/sitter. Lay the cards upon the table in the manner shown below and then you will be ready to decipher your spread:

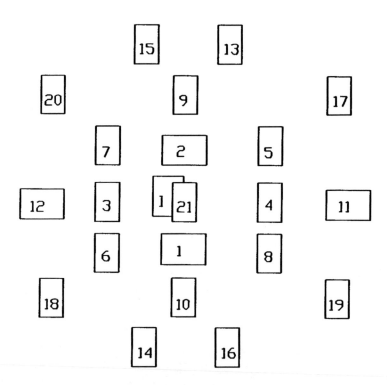

Before looking at each individual position's key meaning, try to fix the usual pattern within your mind, that the cards on the left represent the past and those on the right are the future. Whilst those underneath define your foundations and the cards above, your aspirations; from this you will be able to elucidate upon the card positions to a greater degree.

Key:

Card Position	Topic Covered
1	Inward character
2	Outward character
3	Outdated qualities
4	Continuing qualities
5	Work obstacles
7	Past work achievements
9	Working goals
6	Family connections - background
8	Family connections - current
10	School years. You/personality
12	Past relationships
11	Future relationships
13 & 15	Spiritual aspirations
14 & 16	Hidden personality traits
20	Past religious background
17	Future successes
18	Forgotten abilities
19	Future obstacles
21	How the world sees you!

QABALISTIC

When one has studied the Qabalah fully, there is a method by which the complete 40 Psycard pack may be used, representing the 10 Sephiroth in each of the Four Worlds (ie. drawing the four Trees independently = 40 visible positions). It is naturally noted that in working with the complete 40 Psycards and the entire Qabalistic spread there is always a need to omit Daath.

Obviously, there is a necessity for a full understanding of each Sephirah together with the Pillars and Triangles, etc., in their individual Trees plus each World, to be able to interpret the particular spread at its most lucid translation. There is also a need to lay each Tree independently in order to give its individual clarification within the frame work of the attributes of the specific 'World'. Thus, by leaving all the 'Trees' showing on the table one can finally give a full summary of the Querent's life span to the present time.

By using the Inquirer card together with its own meaning of a maze, you may interpret the symbology quite easily in this spread, ie. should the card, say, land in the position of Malkuth in the World of Assiah the explanation could be that the sitter is a person in a confused state in their material everyday life. Likewise using the 'Yes' and 'No' cards in the same manner it may indicate whether the sitter is imbalanced or actively working correctly within the specific Sephirah that the card lands in.

Naturally, the 'Now" and 'Never" cards may be used in a similar process in addition to using the pictorial description contained within these cards, whereby their interpretational content is expanded (see over for diagrams).

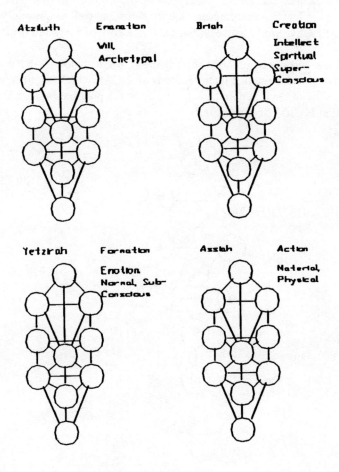

Atzluth   Emanation

Will
Archetypal

Briah   Creation

Intellect
Spiritual
Super-
Conscious

Yetzirah   Formation

Emotion
Normal, Sub-
Conscious

Assiah   Action

Material,
Physical

It must be reiterated that a good sound working knowledge of the Qabalah has to be incorporated within the interpretation of this layout since the basic positions of the cards in any spread determine the individual card's explanation, together with your intuition/psychic abilities.

However, for the 'apprentice' to the Qabalah, it is suggested that once you have an understanding of the basics of the world of Assiah and its relevant Sephiroth's themes, the use of the spread incorporating the first Tree, as follows is excellent for learning the deeper nature as well as putting your knowledge to active working use within the framework of a Psycard reading.

The cards are laid out in order of the Lightning Flash (below). I have also included overleaf the English interpretations of the Attributes, together with the Virtue/Vice of each Sephirah. A brief key to the possible basic position interpretation is also listed opposite.

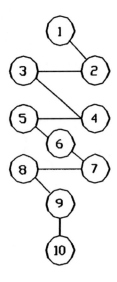

Position			Interpretation
1	Crown	Attainment	The Higher Quest
2	Wisdom	Pure Devotion	Intuition/spiritual drive
3	Understanding	Silence/Avarice	Obstacles and sadness
4	Mercy	Obedience/Tyranny	Wealth and gains
5	Strength	Courage/Destruction	Enemies and arguments
6	Beauty	Devotion to great work/Pride	Fame and Successes
7	Love	Unselfishness/Lust	Love and happiness
8	Splendour	Honesty/Falsehood	Business/Communications
9	Foundation	Independence/Idleness	Health
10	Kingdom	Discrimination/Inertia	Physical Home

Recommended Reading:-

"*Mystical Qabalah*" by Dion Fortune.
"*Kabbalah, Tradition of hidden knowledge*" by Z'ev ben Shimon Halevi.
"*The Talking Tree*" by William Gray.

GAMES

It is always pleasant to be able to while away a few hours with friends and acquaintances in conversation. However, there almost always appears that time when the conversation becomes difficult and you start to run out of words. For this purpose initially I have devised a few 'games' to pass the time and give you added enjoyment of the Psycards.

KNOW YOUR FRIENDS!

Minimum of 2 players - best with a group

The aim is to tell the person directly opposite you about themselves and by this help them to laugh at themselves. Do be light hearted, and do not be afraid to make simple statements within the game as to their style of clothes or colour of hair, etc.

Sitting in an approximate circle with a small table in the middle, shuffle the cards and place them face downwards in the centre. The first player (a) takes a card from the top of the pack and commences to tell the person (b) directly opposite about themselves (b) by using the picture on the card as a guide to the life style and/or personality of player (b). It is advisable to just make one statement in order to limit the time spent with one player at a time. Used cards are placed in a discard pile, and the game continues to move around the players in a clockwise manner.

Variations on this may be brought about in the following way:-

(i)   Using the Inquirer card as a change of direction: reshuffle of deck indicator.

(ii) Using the Direction cards as forfeit cards.

(iii) Using the Direction cards to alter the game as follows:-

    (a)   When a Direction card is taken up the player (a) in question firstly has to pick up the last card laid upon the discard pile and commence to tell truths about him/herself(a) using this discarded card as a guide-line.

    (b)   Then place the two cards upon the discard pile and follow this by picking up a third card but from the fresh pack and continue in the original manner, by "reading" for the player (b) opposite. Thus the player receiving a Direction card has to talk about themselves and player (b) in turn.

THE PSYCHIC ACT!

Minimum of 2 players workable

This game is very similar to the "Know your Friends!" games. It is played by a group of people who accept the possibility that they are psychic or wish to test this theory. Take out the Inquirer and Direction cards and lay them aside. Sitting around in a circle again with a table in the centre, which is about the best position to be in, you are asked to make sure you are comfortable, then close your eyes and meditate on peace and truth. Meditation is quite easy really (to know more, see Meditating with Psycards, later). Just quieten the mind, stop thinking all those little everyday things and concentrate on the one subject. It is suggested that you imagine, initially, a lit candle on the table in front of you and then just think of peace, tranquillity and the word Truth. This need only take a couple of minutes.

Now choose the first player (A) to shuffle the pack whilst concentrating on the player directly opposite (B). Player A takes the top card and uses this as a guide to tell Player B about themselves. The aim is to tell as much as possible whilst using the card as the indicator of the content, but do not be surprised if other thoughts come to mind; these must be given off also. If the Psycards are to be used in the fullest possible way as the key to the Doors of the Mind, you must be prepared for shocks!

Each player shuffles the pack when it is their turn, whilst concentrating upon the person chosen (opposite), continuing in a similar manner. It is suggested that you give a time limit to the 'Reader', since the more psychic you become the longer you can elucidate upon a particular card or person.

Variations on this game:

(i) A larger number of cards to be taken and used by each player, such as 3 or 7.

(ii) If the players to take at least 5 - 7 cards - the Direction cards may be placed back in the deck and used in their correct interpretations.

THE PSYCARDS & NUMEROMANCY SPOOF

Played alone or in a group

Here is a very light-hearted game which you can play with the Psycards and the list below. The number correspondences are thought to be the responsibility of Pythagoras and can be found in the majority of books on Numerology. It must be stressed that this has been designed purely for fun. The complete Pythagoras list has been printed; however, it is fully acknowledged that you will not use the higher numbers, even when using the full variation.

Shuffle the cards whilst pondering upon a question or topic, and then pick three to ten cards, unseen, at random. Turn the cards over and add the numbers together, then look for the respective meaning in the list. Should your number be over 50, separate the units and look up the two figures. However, if the number is over 100, or in the thousands, check the list before working out your calculations as in these examples:-

(a) $25 + 16 + 36 = 77$, i.e. 70 & 7.
(b) $40 + 38 + 39 = 117$, i.e. 100 & 17.

A variation on this game is a 'week ahead' - take seven cards out and add up, repeat this seven times, then make a final total, e.g. 7 cards = 1 total x 7 (days) = 7 totals then added together = 8 totals - one for each day of the week plus a summary.

(c) $141 + 172 + 289 + 122 + 124 + 147 + 130 = 1125$,
       i.e. 1000, 120, 5.

Number   Meanings

1   Ambition, passion, purpose
2   Ruin, Fatality
3   The recognition of God, the soul, destiny
4   Wisdom, strength, power

5	Marriage, happiness
6	Perfected labour
7	Happiness
8	Justice, protection
9	Worry, fallibility
10	Success, future happiness
11	Discord, evasion, lack of integrity
12	City, town, name
13	Injustice
14	Sacrifice, generosity
15	Kindness, integrity
16	Love, happiness, integrity
17	Carelessness
18	Selfishness, callousness
19	Foolishness
20	Wisdom, asceticism
21	Occult wisdom
22	Retribution
23	Prejudice
24	Travel
25	Intelligence, productivity
26	Humanitarianism
27	Resoluteness, bravery
28	Love
29	News, information
30	Marriage, recognition, fame
31	Desire for acclaim
32	Marriage
33	Good fortune
34	Actions in life determine condition in following lives
35	Kindness, gentleness, serenity, charm
36	Genius, an advanced consciousness of being
37	Faithfulness
38	Spite, Avarice
39	Distinction, respect
40	Celebrations, a wedding
41	Shame, dishonour
42	Anxiety, possible ill health
43	Spiritual awareness
44	Happiness and prosperity

45	Descendants
46	Abundance
47	A long and happy life
48	Good taste and judgement
49	Greed
50	A great improvement in circumstances
60	A temporary separation from a loved one
70	Knowledge, wisdom, intuition
75	Material pleasures
77	Repentance, forgiveness
80	Restoration to health
81	Great knowledge and wisdom
90	Temporary problems and set-backs
100	Divine favour
120	Commendation, honour
200	Fear, uncertainty, indecision
215	Misfortune
300	Love of wisdom
318	God's messenger
350	Hope, justice
360	Home, fellowship
365	Astrology, astronomy
400	Long journeys
490	Spiritual advancement
500	Spiritual awareness
600	Spiritual and material perfection
666	Malevolence, conspiracy, vindictiveness
700	Authority, power
800	Victory
900	Quarrels, war
1000	Compassion
1095	Caution, restraint
1260	Anxiety
1390	Dejection

CASE NOTES

This chapter I have found difficult to put together in a manner which is as simple to understand as I trust the rest of this book is. I have decided to be very brief in comments as this section is meant only to be a guide-line as to how the cards may fall in actual 'play'. Therefore, you will find at the beginning of each example a short resume of details gained after the Reading, which will help you to see why it was correct and acceptable to the Querent. I suggest you get the Psycards out and lay them in front of you on the table in the relevant positions to assist your recognition of each situation.

A) **Don** had the opportunity to go self-employed on contract, but he also had to do a probationary training period first, and before the new company would decide whether to give him the contract! He was wondering if he could just take leave from the present employers for the training period - just in case the contract did not transpire!

Arrow Head Spread

Position	Card	Interpretation
I	Birth	New job offer
2	Voyage	Lot of past experience
3	Skills	Variety of suitable abilities
4	Union	Coming together of self
5	Prison	Feeling trapped at present
6	Sun	Success
7	Wheel	Forward movement
8	Death	Answer - positive finish to present job.

Additional intuition gave that the passage into the new job had to be from a clean break; if not it would ultimately go against Don.

B) **Alan**, in his late thirties, has a daughter of 16, with whom he has always had a good relationship, but suddenly she wants to leave home.

Pyramid Spread

Position	Card	Interpretation
1	Home	Stability but leads to next card
2	Prison	A feeling of being trapped
3	Moon	Awakening to need for change
4	Libido	Awakened awareness of self
5	Skills	Need to expand
6	Tower	Inner strength and determination
7	Stranger	Third party influence
8	Tree	Growth of self sought
9	Beast	Obstinance
10	Stars	New cycle.

Further intuition gave that the young lady is growing up quicker than her father realises and thus feels old enough to choose the people she wishes to live with. She would finally leave.

C) **Jill**' - her husband has become withdrawn; she wants to know why.

Pyramid Spread

Position	Card	Interpretation
1	Work	The key to the problem
2	Cave	Emotions shown as depressed
3	Peace	Seeking tranquillity
4	Body	Needs release of tension
5	Wheel	Requires change
6	Liar	Deceiving self in hiding needs
7	Fool	Wants to move away
8	Fortune	Longing for comforts of life
9	Death	Wants complete work change
10	Money	Needs to seek within to find what he wants to do.

D) **Robert** - here we have a materialistic gentleman who came just to test whether there was any fallibility in readings. He is a financial controller and investments consultant, as he finally advised me!

The Cross Spread

Question 'What was his line of business'

Position	Card	Interpretation
1	Union	Control of various elements
2	Voyage	Lot of movement/travel
3	Sage	Commerce and lot of bank dealings
4	Tree	Study of background and knowledge
5	Mother	Caring about needs of others.

Overall picture gave a business man, involved in investments and control of clients' assets, but with a genuine nature and travelled a lot.

E) **Jean** - in a general reading, the following layout showed the loss of a baby. Jean was relieved to be able to talk to a stranger about her emotions, which she had found impossible to speak to family about.

The Cross Spread

Position	Card	Interpretation
1	Union	A coming together
2	Beauty	Looking back on event
3	Puzzle	Worried
4	Birth	The physical event
5	Destruction	The disaster.

F Avril is very heavily involved in spiritual work and condescended to give me a question in order to test this particular layout. Afterwards Avril admitted she had been sterilised a few years previously!

Arrow Head Spread

Question - 'Would she physically have any more children'

Position	Card	Interpretation
1	Peace	Spiritual Quest, Spirituality, Peace and tranquillity within but passes these on
2	Moon	Reflects changes in moods and of past circumstances
3	Death	States finality in the past, finish of ability - bearing question in mind.
4	Skills	Past and current reasons for changes in work becoming overriding obstacle in ability to bring question to fruitful answer
5	Prison	Underlying factor - children restrict movement, progression; past and present

6	Tower	Implies growth of strength and foundations in life, added to other cards indicates growth in work
7	Tree	Past restrictions being overcome; pushing forward fresh branches to assist card 6
8	Cave	Absolute answer - depression due to inability to have another child.

G) Terance was worried about a new job with a lot of responsibility and a move to a new area. He wanted to know if he could achieve success and perhaps receive advice on how to change to meet with this challenge.

Grand Star Spread

Position	Card	Interpretation
1	Now	Present reviewed
2	No	Want things to happen - got to change for success, but very negative on outlook
3	Never	Serious work needed on character
4	Union	Love, how you give to others; got to give without expecting similar back
5	Libido	Energy drives - do not always channel correctly, work for a goal but you put all into achieving goal too quickly - pace
6	Warrior	Trying to prove yourself - male aspect links to father figure
7	Prison	Feel restricted as soon as you get a job that gives foundation and stability
8	Stranger	Apprehensive of somebody walking through door and taking all away
9	Friendship	Achievement in a friendly atmosphere
10	Liberation	Always trying to escape, do not like conformity, restrictions and discipline
11	Liar	Apprehensive of future relationships Afraid of interest shown to you
12	Voyage	Contacts with foreign peoples
13	Money	Dislike of working for money - stay true to your inner self

14	Beast	Hard exterior (mostly hidden) but use it as energy drive.
15	Stars	Seeking change in understanding of higher things
16	Wheel	Wanting movement and change
17	Scales	Balance, look to future
18	Skills	Not used at present, forgotten them, stretch yourself
19	Destruction	Starting afresh, past hanging around
20	Message	Variety of teachings taken in
21	Body	Show yourself as somebody who is vital, pulsating with energy. Energy, drive, success, fight on regardless.

H) Joy is a single person of 36 who is confused with life, thoughts and bad relationships. She wanted guidance on changing her potential.

Fan Spread

Position	Card	Interpretation
1	Peace	Gentle, cushioned, protected childhood
2	Wheel	Change in thoughts and attitudes separation from parents in teens
3	Scales	Life will even out more about age 45 (intuition also gave concern over father's health, mother's eyes and sister's chest)
4	Liberation	Felt suffocation, broke away (late teens)
5	Libido	Sensuality awoken late, gaining control over self
6	Beauty	Stop comparing self with others
7	Moon	Illusions on life and emotional levels caused by childhood
8	Prison	Trapped by emotions due to breakup
9	Money	Trying to dig within self
10	No	Sunday school but no real religious growth or teaching
11	Voyage	Over last 7/8 years increasing growth and questing

12	Death	Will be a sudden, irrevocable change
13	Union	Loves work, but of late something missing
14	Yes	Time to change job, it is mentally stretching but not spiritually or emotionally satisfying
15	Skills	Need to expand skills
16	Tower	Make self, life and property more stable in future. Important changes
17	Home	Change of home next year
18	Sage	Studies and legal connections
19	Now	Will be cutting away facets after reflecting on teachings and then there will be the harvest of self
20	Fortune	Increase in finances, also there will be a step in the future which will feel like backward move but is in reality an upward movement
21	Mother	Yes, you will become a mother and it will happen when you least expect it.

I) **Ron** specifically wished to know if a new business offer should be accepted, whether he should stay where he was and what would develop within the spiritual aspects.

Pascal's Triangle Spread

Position	Card	Position	Card
1	Warrior	2	Moon
3	Money	4	Libido
5	Wheel	6	Death
7	Destruction	8	Message
9	Work	10	Fool
11	Tower	12	Stranger
13	Liar	14	Friendship
15	Skills	16	Union
17	Stars	18	Yes
19	No	20	Peace
21	Voyage	22	Father

23	Sun	24	Tree
25	Scales		

This shows a person whose present path is not good but that the new material path could be if it is confidently followed. This also shows that there is a lot of spiritual/psychic ability but the person always ends up backing off of this path and opts for the material one.

Therefore, the new job should be accepted and discipline is needed within the spiritual aspirations if he is to achieve anything worthwhile.

J) This example is here to show you how to develop a spread yourself. Lyn is married with a large family and wished to know how her children would proceed in life. Since she had seven children, I laid only four cards for each:

17 Year Old - Girl

Card	Interpretation
Yes	Difficulties with studies; needs perseverance.
Message	Needs goals for success.
Friendship	Prefers to be out and about.
Beast	Own worst enemy; needs discipline.

15 Year Old - Boy

Star	Already planned future.
Voyage	Travel and forces.
Wheel	Constant movement.
Work	Career.

13 Year Old - Girl

Tower	Determination.
Money	Does not like to study at school.
Fool	Wants to be out and about.
Prison	Difficult time ahead.

Death	Difficult entry into the world.
Stranger	Feels different to others.
Union	Compassion for world.
Warrior	Fights for others.

8 Year Old - Girl

Beauty	Strong Will.
Sage	Easy to study.
Puzzle	Good concentration but not sure what to study.
Fortune	Success.

5 Year Old - Boy - Twin

Tree	Quiet and thoughtful.
Peace	Gentle nature.
Moon	Secretive.
Birth	Will help others to a new life style.

5 Year Old - Girl - Twin

Now	Lively and vital.
Cave	Causes tension.
Liberation	Own Will.
Body	Will be interested in health aspects.

K) **Mark** (37, Cancerian, married, two children) has been under stress for quite a few years, resulting in distrust of people and life.

Pillars of Life Spread

Position	Card	Interpretation
1	Father	Guiding nature, but fights
2	Libido	Needs self awareness
3	Tower	Shields self

178

4	Liar	Distrust
5	Stars	Goals
6	Beauty	Love of beauty and gentleness
7	Skills	New abilities
8	Warrior	Past pressure - father figure
9	Liberation	New path
10	Fortune	Upward swing
11	Mother	Own passionate nature
12	Death	Closing of old ways
13	Peace	Tranquillity

Summary of physical side	Freedom for future Opportunities
Summary of True Self	Self deception
Summary of Spiritual side	New pattern, partners and skills.

14	Yes	Become positive in outlook
15	Union	Love and harmony coming
16	Cave	Loneliness
17	Puzzle	Choices and confusion again
18	Work	Movement
19	Message	Unexpected knowledge
20	Sun	Relaxation needed
21	Wheel	Break down inner barriers
22	Money	Barrenness; need to dig within
23	Friendship	Relaxation on a social level
24	Never	Cancerian negativity
25	Voyage	Discoveries
26	Home	New home
27	Stranger	Find new self and strength
28	No	Continued retreat from spiritual path
29	Now	New path with a chance to grow
30	Beast	Conquer self, stop negativity for all time
31	Moon	Sudden new psychic abilities/awareness

Question: 'What does it mean?'

Cards   Body, Fool, Birth, Destruction, Sage, Scales and Tree

Answer Lot of work away from present home. Cut away from past. Things will balance out and do not shut yourself away from the more knowledgeable areas.

Unspoken Question

Card   Prison

Answer However, will not necessarily be a happy path - lonely - suggests
       materiality at the expense of spirituality.

(N.B. - 1989. Three years after the above reading Mark's life was exactly as shown in summaries and answers)

Tranquillity and Beyond

Tranquillity is a state of mind, It can only be reached by constant meditation and hard work.

Perseverance is the key word. Keep on trying to calm the mind and stop thought and all sounds heard.

Throw away cares and think of nothing but the Peace of Love and God being ever caring.

Then other feelings, the kind which constantly hide this peace of mind will drop and tranquillity will be known, then from this, one can gather strength of will.

From tranquillity comes an awareness of all life in all forms, an alertness which gives the mind a keen-ness of grasping far more peace but with knowledge at the same moment.

This tranquillity can also give one health and freedom from nervous strain, it can build the power of the mind and give a greater insight into things beyond a physical body.

Direct from Spirit, 1980.

MEDITATING WITH PSYCARDS

I have come to the conclusion, due to my experience of people, travelling around the country carrying out my work over the last few years, that there is not nearly enough meditation taking place. Also, there seem to be a lot of misunderstandings as to its operation. Often, when listening to lectures on the subject, there will be a large number of complicated words and esoteric terminology, which generally totally confuses the beginner or even frightens anyone from becoming a novice.

There are numerous meditational concepts and various approaches to the subject and its practice, which should enable the teachers and lecturers to explain the most suitable path for a particular beginner. However there is the necessity to be able to assess the most suitable terminology to use in order to assist the beginner fully to understand the method and practice. Unfortunately, this last statement is rarely perceived by those who are explaining the subject.

There are also a variety of misconceptions and wrong impressions perceived by the general public, namely that meditation is solely a part of a yoga discipline, or practised only by those seeking a "religious" path and taken often to be no more than a drop out's excuse for inactivity.

However, recently there has been evidence to show that the medical professions are investigating meditation as part of a course of treatment for some patients who have symptoms of stress, whether due to physical ill-health or everyday pressures of life, There are also some hospital practitioners who are conducting controlled tests of this form of treatment, including the use of machines which can register pulse rate changes, etc., such as a sensitivity registering machine which give readouts that can be easily charted by the practitioner or patient. There is at least one hospital in London which has been experimenting with the use of meditation in the maternity department, for expectant mothers suffering with high blood pressure. In recent years, relaxation classes have flourished again all over the country, but mainly as part of antenatal classes or psycho-analysis/therapy courses. Relaxation is also a form of meditation and a way of getting into the habit of gentle meditation as a routine practice. When this forms an accepted part of one's life style, it becomes an automatic method of self-calming and can then be used for a multitude of purposes.

Meditation is a term for the altered states of consciousness which are controlled by exercises and are brought about by the spoken word, picture patterns such as mandalas or yantras; music or chanting mantras etc.; the choice is the participants. Whatever process is used, it is necessary to practice regularly and persistently, although gently, especially in the early days, until the actual art of meditation is perfected.

Meditation can be practised by all and is useful for all ages, from the young child who is hyperactive to the elderly patient who needs revitalising. It has no religious barriers, is performed world wide and has many advantages - inner peace, mental control, emotional stability, spiritual awareness, as an energising process, regression, psychic awakening; to assist concentration, release tension, give personal insight and so on, to give just a few therapeutic uses.

Within the concepts of this book I am going to try and help you to use the psycards as a practical pictorial aid to meditation. As you will have no doubt seen by glancing ahead through the pages of this chapter, I have written down in words the mental journey for your meditation as a suggested thought pattern, whilst you look into the actual card. Obviously once you have studied the relevant picture long enough to be able to remember it, you will be instructed to lay it down and close your eyes, should you prefer, to go on your voyage of discovery. To my mind, the art of meditation and the explanation of how to meditate should be simple and clear, without fabrication, in order that all understand what is required from the beginning, so that the process is successful from the onset.

The sensations felt in the various stages of the process of altering the states of your consciousness (meditation) when analysed are exceptionally like those which can be perceived between the stages of the full awakened state and that of just beginning to fall asleep. Often in the lighter levels of meditation, the beginner disbelieves that they have actually meditated - until they finish and stand up, since it can also be perceived as being similar to the sensations of daydreaming. However, on standing up suddenly after returning even from a light meditative state, the beginner will soon realise that they have not just been "daydreaming" really, since they may feel a little swimmy, light headed, giddy or even disorientated. From this you will realise that it is important not to stand up too quickly after practising meditation until you have "closed down" - that is, brought yourself back to the normal state.

Meditation is simply gently concentrating on a specific topic and each time your mind wanders off to everyday subjects, you bring it back to the topic and start again. When you can concentrate upon a topic for five minutes, start extending the time allowed, and once you can achieve fifteen minutes controlled concentration you have learnt to meditate; then the topic can be changed.

Before continuing I would take this opportunity of expressing my personal suggestion that at what ever level of meditation you intend to practice, you should be aware of the need for protection. Although those of you who have purchased this book just out of curiosity and are not interested in the psychic side may think I am not keeping to the subject, I assure you this paragraph is also for you. Any state of altered awareness opens your psychic centres (see chapter on Assisting Psychic Development, later) therefore, protection is required. In this instance, may I suggest something simple prior to meditation such as a prayer either spoken aloud or silently, e.g:

"Universal Spirit may the Omnipresent Light shine over and protect me."

The preparation and procedure for meditation is as follows; firstly, make sure that anyone in your home at the time you are going to meditate is aware of this fact, then take the telephone off the hook, since if you are surprised suddenly and shocked out of your meditation it will be just like being awoken suddenly from a deep sleep state. This is all common sense protection! Now settle yourself down in a chair with your legs uncrossed and hands resting gently in your lap, palms downwards , have the card which you have chosen in front of you and tell yourself clearly in your mind that you will be meditating only for a specific time, such as 5, 15 or 30 minutes. When you have visualised the picture for long enough you may place it down and continue. It is suggested that you write down your memories for interpretation.

1. The Inquirer

To use this card, look at the colours and pattern, decide which level of yourself you wish to unravel and allow your eyes to drop into the pattern whilst questioning your inner self, then just quieten your mind and allow the allegory to develop over your allotted time. When you arrive back, rest, then go over the journey and try to interpret it for yourself, perhaps making a record for later investigation.

3. No

If you are in need of energy, sit with this card in front of you and concentrate on the red by imagining its energy flowing into your body, but after spending about ten minutes on this, follow it by drawing the blue over yourself and inwards to balance.

6. Body

An interesting theme for a meditation is the Body card which can help you go within yourself. Put the card in front of you and study the design, look to the feet and begin to go within the toes of the left foot - feel yourself inside your own toes, then slowly work your way up the inside of your leg to the body. Creep up the body slowly on the left side inspecting and looking for any dis-ease; if you find any dark patches, they indicate the dis-ease; concentrate on lightening them - cleaning up. Before moving on, go right up to the head and down the right side, not forgetting the arms, until you find yourself back at the toes but on the right foot. Come out of your body to the card and out of the meditation. Take some deep breaths and stretch before moving about too much.

10. Money

Go for a walk in the Money card. Imagine yourself as the farmer ploughing his field on a winter's day, stop and look around, notice the bare trees, look out over the land, leave the plough and walk over the furrows - see something glinting in the earth, stop and pick it up and study what it is. What does it mean to you? Retrace your steps as you come out of your meditation.

11. Friendship

Study the card well, remember all the facets and decide what you want to learn from it before you enter the picture - perhaps become the parrot and listen to the conversations. Await the arrival of the fourth person and then see how the relationships develop. Remember to draw back from being the parrot before you come out of the meditative state.

13. Father

In this meditation, become the child and listen again to the advice of the father and feel his love towards you. Or become the father and learn what it is like to have a father's responsibility.

15. Birth

With this card, quietly allow yourself to become the earth and feel the energy flowing through the different levels. Sense the full growth of new life soaring through you. Become a bulb and grow upwards towards the sunlight, feel the warmth. But remember, of course, to retrace your journey before coming out of the card, and the meditation.

16. Death

Study the card fully before you start. Walk up the pathway towards the entrance to the mound, stand firmly within your own lights, step in the mound and see where you are led. At the end of your journey, return through the same entrance, walk down the pathway into yourself again.

17. Libido

Often there is a need to meditate just in order to relax and feel at peace. Choose in that case this card. Imagine yourself taking a walk in a beautiful garden with nature abounding all around, you are at one with nature so there is no danger even from the snake. Walk to the waterfall and bathe beneath its refreshing life force. Sit awhile on the stones with your feet in the water and let the tension slip away. Gently return from your joyful journey to the awareness of your room.

19 Peace

At times there is a need to go within too find oneself and God, so gaze at this card a while before you close your eyes, relax and then find yourself in the vaulted centre chamber of a cathedral, the sunlight pouring in through the stained glass window while you sit down and rest. As you do, there is a distant choir singing gently, and you are filled with peace and love. At this point accept the love of God; after a while return from this state to your normal awareness.

20. The Sun

Imagine yourself as a butterfly and slip into the picture of this card. Notice the warmth of the Sun, the smell of the ripe corn and then fold your wings and rest upon a flower. Hear the laughter of the children, then allow yourself to wander around the fields noting what you see. After some time, settle on a flower again and then gently become aware of the fact that you are coming out of your meditation and be conscious of your physical self again.

22. The Stars

Study the card and finally imagine yourself getting into a spaceship and setting off to the stars. When you arrive you realise that you are quite safe and get out of your ship for a time, noticing all the colours and light around. To return, get back into your spaceship and retrace your voyage back to your room.

23. The Tree

To use this card, step forward and go into the tree itself; feel its roots and sap and work your way up inside it to the top, coming out above; then look all around noting the scene. Obviously, reverse your journey to return.

24. The Scales

When wishing to use this card you should imagine yourself as the scales and see if you are balanced in your views.

31. The Sage

There are many journeys into meditation that you can take with the use of this card and obviously there is the necessity to decide which one you will go upon before you commence. As a suggestion - slip into the card by becoming the sage yourself and then take a book from the shelf and read. But remember to place the book back upon the shelf before you leave the picture to become yourself.

35. The Voyage

Once again, there is a necessity with this card to decide upon which voyage you will take in your meditation prior to entering the card. You must decide whether it is a spiritual or physical level one, past or future, to another land or even universe. Then join your ship and set sail but, of course, reverse your journey to get back to the present and your physical - normal - self.

36. The Puzzle

An exceptionally interesting card to use as the meditational subject. Initially imagine yourself on a clear day looking at the ground and find beneath your feet the chequered floor. Commence to walk slowly forward, beginning to notice the pattern of the trees overlaid on the chequered design; then let your eyes lift to see the rest of the view all around you. As you continue to step forward, watch the Queen and notice any changes; will she give you guidance as to which door her key opens - or does it actually open both, thus leaving the choice to you again? Go through the door, taking note of all you experience. Spend some time behind the door, but on your return journey be sure to close and lock it, returning the key to the Queen before you retreat out of the card with your memories.

38. Liberation

A simple card to commence a journey with, but which can be quite fun. Start behind the closed door, open it and find yourself suddenly upon a horse with another, racing down the road across the bridge - now who are you with and where are you going? These questions, together with their answers, fill the rest of your journey. However, as always you must retrace your steps and close the door behind you before coming out of this card, this will ensure that you do return to your normal level of consciousness.

39. The Cave

To help you set your own meditations, use the Cave as a starting point and then either go deeper, or walk through the opening and see what you might see.

Of course, this final method can be of use with all the cards and therefore, I wish you total enjoyment in your meditations whatever the journey may be; however, always remember to retrace your early steps to come out of a meditation, then stretch, breathe deeper and have a drink of water and a biscuit.

Blessings

Berenice.

ASSISTING PSYCHIC DEVELOPMENT

There are many aids to psychic development, and Psycards may also be used; however, it is of course necessary to understand what the psychic faculties actually are.

You have in the simplest terms a physical body and a spiritual self and the doorway between the two is the psychic self. The psychic faculties initially are the extension of your everyday ones - sight, sound, smell, taste, touch and thought. Clairvoyance is "clear seeing" - the sight; either a picture or 'being' in the air around you, then again it can be just like a television set inside your forehead. Clairaudience is obviously to do with the hearing abilities, and again this can be a voice inside or outside of your head. Clairsentience is the sensing and feeling of changes in the environment around you and within your own body, such as emotions at the time of attuning yourself to the other dimensions. The sense of smell, tasting and touch, therefore, all come under the title of clairsentience.

The ability of thought comer under the heading of Mental Impression; it is just like intuition.

Now, there are also other abilities which are heard of and may come your way, although they are much rarer in this day and age, i.e. Materialisation (physical build up of an entity); Direct Voice (an audible voice - heard by all present); Transfiguration (a face being seen over the top of the medium's features) and Trance. However, materialisation and direct voice abilities only come about via a medium possessing the trance faculty. Trance is the altered state of consciousness being achieved to a high degree whereby another persona flows information directly through the medium's vocal chords.

Now, to use the pictorial imagery of the Psycards to enhance your psychic attunement, it will be necessary for you initially to allow yourself a set appointment and an appropriate length of time weekly, whereby you sit specifically with this purpose in mind from the moment you sit down during your allotted time to the moment you close; no thought or sense is to be considered your own. Always keep a diary of what has occurred (or not) so that after a few months you can read it back and assess your progress properly.

In most cases at the beginning the picture on your chosen Psycard will be the clairvoyant picture for you to interpret. Naturally, it is much easier to develop abilities within a group, but if alone, follow my suggestions of a diary explicitly. As with the meditation exercises, ask or protection before you commence any of these exercises.

1. Do a general reading for yourself just using the cards which appear as the message and put it into words as if you were talking to another person, thus not about yourself - this will help you to stand back from your own situation. If you meditate gently first, it will assist you to be detached from yourself in this exercise.

2. Choose a card which you have a dislike for, or have always avoided, and meditate upon the imagery - allow yourself to go within and contemplate on the picture's effect upon yourself.

3. Use the cards as triggers to your abilities by just visualising the picture and asking for guidance in your spiritual path, and then write down the thoughts that come. Do not be surprised if the thoughts finally flow quicker than you can write - this becomes Inspirational Writing. Alternatively, use a tape recorder and speak the words aloud, thus you will have commenced Inspirational Speaking.

4. Choose a card and then ask for spirit guides to come close - you will no doubt find one come who can easily be associated with the archetypal characteristics displayed in the card. Notice the changes in your own body, such as whether you feel larger or smaller, does your heart beat faster? Perhaps you feel a little giddy? Unfortunately, not all the sensations that spirits bring forward initially are pleasant; it takes time tor us to get used to the metaphysical changes just as it does for them to adjust to us.

5. Select a card and ask for a loved one to come close. Just hold the card and wait for changes to occur in yourself. Although you may suddenly become clairvoyant or clairaudiant, it should be remembered that everyone is also born with the natural ability to be sensitive, so note the changes. Perhaps they are giving you the sensations of the actual conditions of their passing. If you notice a change accept it by making a mental note of the sensation and more information will follow.

Naturally, just using the cards in the normal way will open your psychic self eventually, whether you fully appreciate this or not, since the whole design and concept of the Psycards is aimed at a greater awareness of your Self.

A further way to assist your understanding of your own Self is to ask friends to participate with you in the Psychic Game, but instead of asking them to take turns in interpreting the cards, you interpret for each of them in turn. Thus you get the practice in noticing how you "receive" and they can test you.

A card such as the Inquirer may be used as a trigger to your psychic self, this being the only card used to gain all manner of information - use it as the focal point for concentration in a meditative state first, then allow the intuition to flow and just continue to write or say what comes to mind. This is similar to the way one uses a crystal ball.

Whichever method you try I wish you a safe and exciting journey; however, if a query arises which cannot be answered by a medium/psychic residing locally to yourself, I am willing to give advice (if you allow me time), and you may write to me c/o the publisher, or the British Astrological and Psychic Society (BAPS), enclosing a stamped addressed envelope for your reply.

A selection of other Capall Bann titles. Free catalogue available.

Tarot Therapy vol 1 - Tarot for the New Millennium by Steve Hounsome

A groundbreaking new work proposing the use of the Tarot as a therapy, alongside the many other complementary and natural procedures available. This largely ignored method of working with and viewing the cards begins the work of restoring the Tarot to its rightful place of acceptance as a sacred healing tool. This first of three volumes, '*Tarot for the New Millennium*', explains the theory behind the idea of Tarot Therapy, tracing its origins and history in this light. The concept of both Major and Minor Arcanas are explored, showing the true, therapeutic construction of the pack. The book outlines methods of working with the Tarot as a therapy in consultations, adding many other ways in which it can be utilised in this manner. Volume 2 will contain an exploration of the Major Arcana cards in their therapeutic setting and use and Volume 3 will do the same for the Minor Arcana. This major new work on the Tarot represents a turning point in its evolution, which the author shows has always adapted itself to the needs of humanity since its inception Here is the method of working with the Tarot in the Aquarian Age, above and beyond its current position. ISBN 186163 074 3

The Inner Space Work Book
Developing Counselling & Magickal Skills Through the Tarot
by Cat Summers & Julian Vayne

Psychic & personal development using the tarot, pathworkings & meditations; exploring techniques as varied as shamanism, bodymind skills & ritual, through the medium of the tarot. Two pathways interweave through the text. One concentrates on the development of psychic sensitivity, divination & counselling, as well as discussing their ethics & practical application. The other leads the student deeper into the realm of Inner Space, exploring the Self through meditation, pathworking, physical exercises & ritual. Both paths weave together to provide the student with a firm grounding in many aspects of the esoteric. A 'user friendly' system for unlocking all your latent magickal talents. ISBN 898307 13X   £9.95t

Self Enlightenment by Mayan O'Brien

Are you on a quest for truth, knowledge and wisdom? If so, this book will be a guide and a stepping stone for you. *Self Enlightenment* is full of practical advice on many areas of life. It discusses meditation, visualisation, the aura, examining our lives, creating a mind map, using astrology, the University of the solar System (a guided visualisation), the Tree of Life, health and herbs and how to organise a retreat for yourself. This book can be seen as a beacon to illuminate your way. ISBN 186163 0484   £9.95

The Face of the Deep - Healing Body and Soul by Penny Allen

We cannot truly heal our bodies or minds without recognising the needs of the soul. The healing process appears magical or miraculous only when we do not understand the inner workings behind life. Outer and inner are inseparable. Ancient gods share their names with the planets and their influences with colours, music, numbers and chakras, the energy wheels within our bodies. Penny Allen has a background as a journalist and a teacher of literature as well as twenty years of experience as a teacher of meditation and as a healer, counsellor and astrologer. Drawing on mythology, she leads us on a fascinating journey of discovery showing how the soul is linked to the body and mind and concluding that, if we are to heal ourselves and our environment, we must align ourselves once again to the universe of which we are part. ISBN 186163 0409   £9.95   **R98**

FREE DETAILED CATALOGUE

A detailed illustrated catalogue is available on request, SAE or International Postal Coupon appreciated. **Titles can be ordered direct from Capall Bann, post free in the UK** (cheque or PO with order) or from good bookshops and specialist outlets. Titles currently available include:

Angels and Goddesses - Celtic Christianity & Paganism by Michael Howard
Arthur - The Legend Unveiled by C Johnson & E Lung
Auguries and Omens - The Magical Lore of Birds by Yvonne Aburrow
Book of the Veil The by Peter Paddon
Caer Sidhe - Celtic Astrology and Astronomy by Michael Bayley
Call of the Horned Piper by Nigel Jackson
Celtic Lore & Druidic Ritual by Rhiannon Ryall
Earth Dance - A Year of Pagan Rituals by Jan Brodie
Earth Magic by Margaret McArthur
Enchanted Forest - The Magical Lore of Trees by Yvonne Aburrow
Familiars - Animal Powers of Britain by Anna Franklin
Healing Homes by Jennifer Dent
Herbcraft - Shamanic & Ritual Use of Herbs by Susan Lavender & Anna Franklin
In Search of Herne the Hunter by Eric Fitch
Magical Guardians - Exploring the Spirit & Nature of Trees by Philip Heselton
Magical Lore of Cats by Marion Davies
Magical Lore of Herbs by Marion Davies
Masks of Misrule - The Horned God & His Cult in Europe by Nigel Jackson
Patchwork of Magic by Julia Day
Psychic Self Defence - Real Solutions by Jan Brodie
Sacred Animals by Gordon MacLellan
Sacred Grove - The Mysteries of the Forest by Yvonne Aburrow
Sacred Geometry by Nigel Pennick
Sacred Lore of Horses The by Marion Davies
Sacred Ring - Pagan Origins British Folk Festivals & Customs by Michael Howard
Seasonal Magic - Diary of a Village Witch by Paddy Slade
Secret Places of the Goddess by Philip Heselton
Talking to the Earth by Gordon Maclellan
Taming the Wolf - Full Moon Meditations by Steve Hounsome

Capall Bann is owned and run by people actively involved in many of the areas in which we publish. Our list is expanding rapidly so do contact us for details on the latest releases.

Capall Bann Publishing, Freshfields, Chieveley, Berks, RG20 8TF